THE
BABYSITTER'S
HANDBOOK

THE BABYSITTER'S HANDBOOK

Barbara Benton

WILLIAM MORROW AND COMPANY, INC.

New York   *1981*

Library of Congress Cataloging in Publication Data

Benton, Barbara.
    The babysitter's handbook.

    Includes index.
    1. Baby sitters.   I. Title.
HQ769.5.B45   649′.1′0248   81-3996
ISBN 0-688-00641-8   AACR2
ISBN 0-688-00687-6 (pbk.)

Printed in the United States of America

First Edition

        4   5   6   7   8   9   10

BOOK DESIGN BY MICHAEL MAUCERI

To Elaine and Robin, my best sitters

CONTENTS

7

INTRODUCTION

You've decided to be a babysitter. To you, the benefits will be the satisfactions of earning an income and of providing a valuable service. You will learn something about work and the world of business, and you will find out what it is to be responsible for another person. What you experience as a babysitter will help you in the future, whether you decide to have a family, a career, or both.

To your employers, the parents you sit for, the benefit will be a few hours of freedom from the demands of child-rearing. Child-rearing is tremendously rewarding; it can also be exhausting and confining. To stay fresh, to keep loving it, in order to be at their best, parents sometimes need time away from their children: They need to be alone with each other, to go out with friends, to pursue adult interests, or sometimes, once in a while, just to do the shopping quickly or take a nap without interruption.

Parents want to know that while they are absent their children are being well cared for—that they are with a kind-hearted and loving person who will, with dependability and good humor, keep them safe, cuddle them, play with them, feed them, bathe them, and put them to bed. The more confident and aware parents are of your abilities, the more relaxed they can be while they are away from their children, and the more valuable you will be to them as a sitter. The more valuable you are, the more in demand you will be. You will have greater satisfaction from a job well done, a greater selection of jobs to choose from, and you will be justified in asking for a higher hourly rate. In short, you will be a successful sitter.

12

This book is meant to help you achieve success. Areas of information are grouped into chapters, which are divided into topics with subheads. When you need to know something, you can look it up in the emergency index on the back cover, the more general index inside, or the table of contents. It is a book that is meant, too, to be written in. The last chapter is a log where you can jot down your own notes about specific jobs and keep a permanent record of your work. It is your book, to be used as a tool in your profession.

Emphasis is on the care of babies, toddlers, and older, but still preschool-age, children. School-age children often do need sitters, but by this age children are highly communicative and self-directed. When parents are away, they need an older person in the house with them for safety and some direction, but they take pride in their capacity to care for themselves. They are not so far apart in age and ability from the sitter "herself."

Herself appears in quotes above to emphasize the problem of pronouns. For the last several years confusion among writers persists concerning the use of pronouns that indicate a person's gender: he, she, him, her, his, and hers. When the person written about could be either male or female, when is it appropriate and fair to use which?

In the past, babysitters have been exclusively female. This is changing. As in child-rearing in general, more and more males are finding babysitting an occupation well suited to their temperaments and abilities. This is good because young children need male as well as female influence.

Some writers solve the problem of pronouns by using a mixture. This works but is bothersome

13

and distracting. For the sake of consistency and convenience—and in recognition that, still, most sitters are female—I will refer to the sitter always as *she*. To balance this choice—and for no other reason—the child she cares for will be *he*.

1.  BUSINESS

The government has estimated that about one million young adults babysit in the United States. Most of these sit at least three hours a week, fifty-two weeks a year. It's hard to say what any sitter might earn per hour because that figure varies with a sitter's age and experience and from neighborhood to neighborhood. But if you want a rough estimate of income generated by babysitting in this country each year, multiply one million sitters by three hours by fifty-two weeks by the current minimum hourly rate in your neighborhood. You will get a dollar-figure somewhere up in the millions. Babysitting is *big business*.

Like any other business, it is competitive: The best sitters get the best jobs and earn the most money. It will be to your advantage to go about your business with seriousness, a sense of responsibility, and a sound knowledge of what you are doing.

15

Being in the Right Business

Before you go into the babysitting business you should consider carefully—and honestly—if it is the right job for you. If you enjoy it, if you are good at it, you can pass many pleasant hours while you're earning money. But if you don't really like it, if it's hard for you to get through a job, you can make yourself—and the child you are caring for—miserable.

Consider your attitude toward small children. No one has good feelings toward all children all the time (not even parents!), but you can assess how you feel about children in general. Do you see them as *people*, like you, but vulnerable and inexperienced? Do you think of them as sweet, smart, funny, creative, and adventurous? Do they arouse in you feelings of tenderness and admiration? On the practical side, could you change a messy diaper or help a toddler on and off the toilet with, if not enthusiasm, willingness? Could you keep these positive feelings going—for hours? If so, very likely you will be a good sitter.

On the other hand, do you value children only as cute playthings, fun sometimes but inferior to older people in intelligence and ability? Do you find many of them ill-behaved or annoying? Would you resent being touched with sticky hands or be driven frantic by fifteen minutes of irritable crying? Would you find yourself bored with them after a short time, wishing their parents would come home? That you have these feelings doesn't mean you are a bad person, just that you would not be a good sitter. We aren't all cut out for child care, nor should we be. Put this book down right now and find one on your favorite subject. Try to figure

17

out a way to earn money using the abilities you do have.

Getting Experience

You may think it's a hopeless situation: No one wants to hire you if you have no experience, but you can't get experience unless someone hires you. That's not quite right. You can get experience before you take on complete responsibility for a child.

Younger brothers and sisters—your siblings, or "sibs"—are the best "guinea pigs." If you have younger sibs, you probably have already learned a lot by helping your parents: bathing your little brother while your mother is preparing dinner; singing a lullaby and tucking him into bed while your father washes dishes; or keeping "an ear out" for him as he sleeps, while they both go to a movie. This at-home experience is only one step removed from caring for other people's children. The difference is that you and your younger sib know each other—and your parents know you both—inside out. Any difficulties usually are foreseen and prevented. In any case, help usually is immediately available. Errors are forgiven.

When you begin to babysit outside your home, do so gradually. Start with children near the same age as your sib, preferably those you know, and for only short periods of time. You can widen the age-range and increase the length of time as you gain experience and confidence.

If you have no younger brothers and sisters, you will have to go outside your home for experience. You might begin with the younger children of nearby relatives or friends of your parents. Take every opportunity to spend time with children. When visiting, learn how to play with them. You

18

may think this an obvious thing, but interests and abilities vary as much among small children as they do among your friends. What is fascinating and fun to one may be boring to or beyond the understanding of another. Apart from play, you need to learn how to care for children's needs. Watch as they are being fed, bathed, or put to bed. Ask questions. Volunteer to help in any way you can, even if it's only putting milk into the bottle, holding the towel, or finding the teddy bear. As adults see your interest in children and your ability to be helpful, they will begin to rely on you in little ways. Soon you may find yourself with a request to come over and play with a child while his mother spends an hour at the typewriter, or you may be trusted to stay alone in the house with him for an hour or two while he is asleep.

You can also learn from an older brother or sister or from a friend who is an experienced babysitter. Ask to go along on jobs with this person, so that you can watch and learn. Suggest that in exchange for the favor, you can help care for the children in small ways. Be as good as your word—do not get in the way—and do not ask for payment. Success depends on the quality of your relationship with the older sitter. If it is truly cooperative, this is an excellent, and perhaps the best, way to learn.

From these small beginnings, your experience grows. You can become a "mother's helper," available for relatively short periods of time, in the parents' presence or not, taking on as many responsibilities as you are comfortable with. It may be helpful to team up with a sib or friend near the same age who also is learning the babysitting business. The two of you might accept jobs together that neither could handle alone. This is good,

19

though, only if the two of you truly work well together.

Sometimes things happen too fast. Don't be shy about refusing to take on work you don't feel ready for. If, for instance, after two brief encounters with Tommy, Mrs. Smith presses you to take care of him one Saturday for six hours, during which time he will be wide awake and you will have to give him two meals and a bath, you are entitled to say no. You may tell her that you'd like to get to know Tommy better before you stay with him that long, or that you'd like to wait until you have more experience before you accept that much responsibility. You might soften your refusal by recommending to Mrs. Smith an older or more experienced friend, but don't be tempted by the money or persuaded to do it against your better judgment. Better that you pass up the job than that you and Tommy have a bad experience. Human nature being what it is, if Mrs. Smith comes home and finds you or Tommy or both in tears, there is a good chance she will blame you, not herself. You will lose ground in your relationship with Tommy; you are bound to lose at least a little self-confidence; and the incident will detract from your reputation as a sitter.

Building a Reputation

Your reputation will consist mainly of what parents think of your ability to handle children. Your ability will increase little by little with each job, along with your confidence. Confidence is contagious. When you walk into a job, knowing and self-assured, friendly with both parents and children, asking intelligent questions, making sensible suggestions—you've made it to second base at least.

Parents relax, tell you what you need to know, say good-bye, and leave knowing their children are in good hands. The children sense from their parents' manner and yours that all is well. Barring bad luck, the children will be cheerful and cooperative; you and they will have a good time. Returning to find everyone content, the pleased parents will have good things to say about you to their friends or anyone else needing a sitter.

Your self-confidence is vitally important. You don't want anything to shake it, so never take on a job you aren't sure you can handle.

Apart from your ability to take care of children, your reputation will be made from your business dealings with parents. In this respect, babysitting is like any other business. You need to present yourself as sensible, reliable, fair-minded, and honest. These attributes will be visible—or not—in the way you do business.

Setting Your Hourly Rate

Babysitting rates vary from neighborhood to neighborhood, region to region, depending on the local economy and rate of inflation. What you charge per hour will depend on the range of rates in your neighborhood and on how you stack up against your competitors in age, ability, experience, and reputation.

Ask around to find out what other sitters in your neighborhood charge. Let us say, for the sake of discussion only, that the rates vary from one to two dollars an hour. If you are among the older, abler, experienced sitters, and are highly regarded by the families you sit for, you are justified in asking the maximum of two dollars an hour. If, on the other hand, you are comparatively young, have just begun to babysit, and have not yet built

21

a strong reputation, you would be wise to ask the minimum of one dollar an hour. You can increase your rate by small amounts as you build up experience and ability.

If all your jobs are in the same neighborhood, it is best to be consistent: Charge everyone the same amount. When you decide to raise your rate, tell everyone at once. It is bad politics to charge Mrs. Brown twenty-five cents more an hour than Mrs. Jones, even though Johnny Brown is ten times more difficult to handle than Billy Jones. (There are ways to deal with difficult Johnny. Read chapters on child development and play.) It is an entirely different matter, of course, if Mrs. Brown gives you the raise voluntarily because she recognizes the difficulty and appreciates your patience.

You may charge more per hour if you have more than one child to care for. This increase varies from neighborhood to neighborhood as well, but does not double for two, triple for three, and so on. You might charge roughly time-and-a-quarter for two children and time-and-a-half for three. For example, if your rate were one dollar an hour for one child, it might be a dollar twenty-five for two and a dollar-and-a-half for three.

It is acceptable, too, to ask for payment for any housework you are asked to do, other than routine tidying up after yourself or the child. For example, if Mrs. Jones asks you to wash the dinner dishes, which she and Mr. Jones left in the sink, after Billy is in bed—and if you want to—you can agree to do so for a fee comparable to your hourly rate. That is, if your rate is a dollar an hour, and it takes you half an hour to wash dishes (assuming you're a fair dishwasher and don't dawdle), you might ask fifty cents for doing the dishes. But

22

be sure Mrs. Jones understands this before she leaves.

You should not expect bonuses. Your rate, after all, reflects what you think your work is worth. Bonuses are sometimes given by generous parents who particularly value the care you have given their children. When you receive a bonus, accept it for the gracious compliment that it is.

Advertising

Most of your advertising will be strictly word-of-mouth—your neighborhood reputation. Mrs. Adams, chatting with Mrs. O'Brien in the park, says, "I'm really stuck for good sitters lately. Who are you using?" Mrs. O'Brien replies, "Mrs. Stone tells me that she sometimes uses a new girl named Elizabeth Cruz. Her family just moved here. Mrs. Stone tells me that Elizabeth is very good with the twins." To this, Mrs. Adams answers, "Yes, I've heard some nice things about Elizabeth, too. I think I'll give her a call soon." And so it usually goes.

In newer neighborhoods where young children outnumber young adults, you should have no trouble finding work simply by word-of-mouth advertising. In fact, jobs probably will find you. But in older neighborhoods, where most of the children have grown up to your age or older and have not been replaced with a new set, it will be more difficult for you. You will have to resort to other kinds of advertising and, when you do find work, be willing to travel to other nearby neighborhoods.

The next best thing to word-of-mouth is *free* advertising. First, try putting up notices on community bulletin boards. You find these in neighborhood grocery stores, candy stores, drugstores, churches and synagogues, schools, community

23

centers, swimming pools, laundermats, and the lobbies of apartment buildings. Check around your neighborhood to find out which bulletin boards are most used and try those first, but if you don't get a prompt response, use the other bulletin boards as well. You never know when some out-of-the-way ad will "pull."

Find out if the bulletin boards you want to use really are public—that anyone can use them. It's a waste of time to make a notice that someone in charge will remove the next day. If you aren't sure, ask the store manager, building superintendent, or whomever. Check the size of the notices already there and the space available. You want yours to stand out, but you can't cover up or crowd out everyone else's. Ask if a time limit regulates how long the notice can stay up. Some places, because of the demand for space, ask you to put a date on your notice. When the time limit is up, someone takes the notice down.

After you've decided how many notices and what size, work on a rough draft. Wording is important. Keep in mind that people do not spend much time reading ads. They scan quickly for certain key words. When they find a key word ("Babysitter"), they slow down and read more carefully. The few words you choose must be informative. Tell what you offer, who you are, and where to reach you. Whether or not you include your hourly rate in this or any other ad depends on whether or not you are willing to bargain. If you absolutely are not willing, state your rate.

People who read bulletin boards are usually on their way somewhere and don't have pencil and paper handy. If you're not restricted to a three-by-five-inch card, it's a good idea to have your telephone number written several times on tabs at the bottom of the ad. Precut them (like fringe) so they can tear off easily. For safety reasons, it is best to advertise with only your telephone number.

BABYSITTER

15-year-old boy experienced with infants and toddlers. After school, evenings, weekends. $1.50/hr. References available. 241-6372

MOTHER'S HELPER

12-year-old girl will babysit your child at home or in park. After school, until 5:30 p.m. 744-9867

Be sure your spelling is correct. Print or type neatly, and space your words evenly. Remember that your notice will be someone's first impression of you. You want it to be eye-catching, so use color. You don't have to be an artist to do a good notice, but if you happen to be one, use your talent.

When you're satisfied with your rough draft, crank out however many more you need. If that's just a few, you could do them all by hand; but if you want more and you don't mind spending a few cents on each, you could photocopy them.

25

Print them in black on standard-size paper and run them off. You can add the color (felt-tip pen, crayon, or whatever) later.

If you can manage to get them copied or mimeographed for free (an adult friend who works in an office or school might be a source), you can hand out your notices as circulars, a form of free advertising that takes courage. (If you're doing this many, forget the coloring.) You might hike through your neighborhood and those adjoining and put your circulars into mailboxes or under doors. You can plant yourself outside the door of the elementary school auditorium (or as close as allowed) just before a PTA meeting and hand them to attending parents. The local park, the daycare center, or nursery school are other likely spots to encounter the parents of young children. Others may occur to you. Be prepared to meet some unfriendly people.

If you'd rather and if you have enough money to invest, consider placing a classified ad in your local newspaper or "pennysaver." Word your ad much as you did above, but also specify the neighborhood(s) you are willing to work in. You will want to prevent disappointing telephone calls from people who live too far away for you to consider. Paid advertising reaches many more people over a larger area than the unpaid type.

> BABYSITTER. High-school girl in Kingsbridge area. Experienced with newborn to elementary-school-age children. Evenings only. References available. 998-4523.

26 Before you decide to place an ad, call the prospective publication and ask about their classified ad rates. "Pennysavers" usually are cheaper

than newspapers. Tell them your exact wording (they may give you some advice and help you abbreviate to save space); they will then tell you the cost, which may include a discount if the ad runs (is printed) in more than one issue of the publication. Write the information down, so you don't forget. If the person you are speaking to presses you to place the ad right away, and you aren't sure you want to, politely but firmly insist that you want to think about it. Ask when the deadline is (the last day that you can call), and hang up. No need to rush. It is that person's job to sell ads; it is yours to look after your best interests.

Getting Jobs

Eventually, whatever form of advertising you're using will produce inquiries. People will want to check you out. With word-of-mouth advertising you will most likely know the person who telephones you, drops by for a visit, or stops you on the street to ask about babysitting. In this case, you can assume that he or she is trustworthy. If, however, your advertising reaches someone you don't know, *you must be cautious*.

Before you give your own address or other personal details, get the person's name, address, telephone number, and as much other information as you need to be satisfied with his or her sincerity. Never meet a stranger alone in your home or elsewhere. Never accept a car ride with a stranger. Never accept a job with a stranger without checking up first. If in doubt, ask your parents' advice or ask them to accompany you on an interview. That we have to be this careful is a sad statement about our times; nonetheless it is a reality, especially in big cities.

27

When you are confident about the person you're talking to, by all means be open and informative about the business that concerns you both. Discuss the number of children and their ages. Consider carefully whether you are able to handle them. You will also want to know about transportation. If you live near enough to walk back and forth, you need only to agree upon who will escort you. Particularly late at night, you will want someone to see you right to your door. If you live far enough away to need transportation, it is most usual for one of the parents to pick you up and drop you off by car. Alternatively, parents may pay you extra for bus or cab fare. In all circumstances, consider your safety first. (See note on intoxication, p. 44.)

Your prospective employer will want to know your past experience, your hourly rate, and your availability. Also, as the two of you talk, he or she will notice your manner and the words you choose to express yourself. Be straightforward and honest in your answers to questions—no wishy-washiness.

When talking about your babysitting experience, be specific: "Yes, I've been sitting regularly for the last two years, most of the time for Mr. and Mrs. Patterson and for Mr. and Mrs. Allen, although occasionally for other people as well. The children have been from three-months to six-years-old." Or: "I started sitting last summer for Mr. and Mrs. Levine, whose children are three-and five-years-old. I'd be willing to take care of a younger child, as long as we aren't left for long until we get used to each other."

28

When asked about your hourly rate, look at the person's face; answer without hesitation and with a level voice. If your rate is within the neighborhood range, it will probably be accepted without question. If you happen to be dealing with the type of person who wants a bargain in everything, or if your rate is really a little high, you *might* (although it is not necessary to do so) want to explain how you arrived at that figure. If you've given your rate careful thought, this won't be hard to do: "It's the going rate around here for sitters of my age and experience." Or: "My rate is a little higher than average because, although I'm only fourteen, I have a lot of experience, especially with younger children, and I've also had the Red Cross course in first aid." If the person makes a counter offer or presses you (by saying something like, "I just can't afford to pay you that much"), you must decide whether you will stand firm or lower your rate. If you feel the person is being unfair or if you really don't want to work for the money offered, turn the job down politely: "Sorry, but my rate is firm." Or: "I think you'd be happier with someone else." On the other hand, if you need the work or if you want to do it for less, it's perfectly acceptable to come down. Just be prepared to make adjustments elsewhere (see p. 22).

When discussing your availability, it is very important that you be clear-headed and organized. To help you remember, *get a calendar.* Nothing is more embarrassing than showing up on the wrong day and being greeted by puzzled faces, or being in the middle of a peaceful meal with your family when a frantic parent telephones, "Where are you?!"

The best calendars are the types that allow you to see a week or a month at a glance and give you enough space to write down appointments. Keep your calendar handy, in your school bag or

29

near the telephone, and keep it up to date. Write down not only your babysitting appointments but other happenings as well—music lessons, family outings, and so forth. This way, when someone new wants to know when you're generally available, you can give a very clear answer: "I'm free after school from around 4:00 till 6:00, for the next two weeks, until practice for my school play starts. After that I'll be available on school nights only from 8:00 till 10:30. [You leave two hours free for dinner and homework.] I'm usually free on Friday nights till pretty late." You don't mention Saturday, because you always sit for someone else that night, or Sunday, because you try to save that day for your family. When asked to babysit on a specific date, you simply look to see if it's free. If so, you accept the job and write it on the calendar.

Be careful not to overschedule. You're babysitting, among other reasons, to earn money, and that's a powerful incentive to accept jobs as they are offered. But you can get your schedule so jammed with commitments that all you do is race from one activity to another with never a moment to spend with your family or just to be alone to do as you wish. Sooner or later you'll get tired and irritable. That's not fair to you, to your family, or to the families you sit for. Leave some space on your calendar—and in your life.

A word, too, about loyalties: There are bound to be one or two families who have come to depend on you as their sitter—and on whom, in the past, you have been able to rely for work. Probably you've been with them since you first started babysitting. The children know you well and look forward to your coming. As much as you may want to meet new people and to gain new ex-

30

perience—and if you want to, you surely will—
don't forget these old friends. If you always sit
for a particular family on Saturday nights, for instance, continue to do so. Make yourself available
to new people on Friday nights or some other
time. If a conflict arises—you think a family will
want you for an evening that someone new has
just asked you for, but you're not sure—don't be
embarrassed to ask. (Don't keep the new person
waiting long for your answer, though.) There's
no harm in letting old friends know you're in
greater demand than before. They will appreciate
your thoughtfulness in thinking of them first, and
they may be smart enough to give you a raise!

After discussing these matters, it should be clear
to both you and the parent whether or not arrangements between you can be worked out. If
things look good, perhaps the parent will promise
to call you in the near future, or perhaps he or she
will offer you a job on the spot.

Going to Work

You want a neat attractive appearance—combed
and clean—but you don't want to be overdressed.
Your new silk shirt will not impress the children
and it may prevent you from joining them in active play. Wear comfortable, washable clothing
appropriate to the weather. Before you leave—for
the first or any subsequent babysitting job—write
down for your own family the name, address, and
telephone number of the parents you're working
for, along with the time you expect to be home.

If a family is completely new to you, it is a good
idea to visit with them, at least briefly, before
you sit the first time. You can not only finish up
business, but also meet the children and famil-

31

iarize yourself a bit with the home and family lifestyle before you take over. Often, however, a preliminary visit is not possible, and you must take care of all of these matters the first time you sit. For this reason, and also because you and the children, particularly if they are young, should be allowed to grow used to each other gradually, the first time you sit should be relatively short.

Arrange to arrive about half an hour early. Prepare a list of things (at least in your head, preferably on paper) that you want to discuss with the parents before they leave. The more organized you are, the more quickly you can cover each item and the less likely you will be to forget something important. Your businesslike attitude will assure everyone of your seriousness about your work.

The first item in the order of business is to meet the children and to get your instructions about their care. Bring this book along and use the last chapter, the log, as a notebook. Use this time to get permanent emergency telephone numbers as well as the number where the parents can be reached that evening. Take brief notes to help you remember any special instructions about the children's routine, but don't be so busy writing that you don't hear all that is being said. (That's sometimes a danger in notetaking.) If the parents are talking so fast you can't absorb everything, ask them to slow down or to repeat instructions. It's important that you understand what you are supposed to do. You can fill in your log in more detail later. Right now you are concerned with making your first impression on the family and with receiving general impressions about them.

Familiarize yourself with the home well enough

32

to find what you will need in the way of equipment, food, clothing, and so forth. Tour the kitchen and bathroom. Check out the pets. Find the telephone, paper, and pencil. Are there any calls, visits, or deliveries expected? Ask how to operate the locks, temperature controls, and any appliances you may use. (All of this is covered in greater detail in Chapter 2.)

In the course of conversation, if you have not done so previously, settle with the parents on your hourly rate, transportation, and any other important business matters concerning this visit.

When everyone seems comfortable—*and this should not be rushed*—it is time to say good-bye to the parents. When they have gone, turn your attention fully to the children. (See *Separation*, pp. 78–80.) How you relate to the children and care for their needs is what the rest of this book is about. Draw from it, from your previous experience, and from your instincts. With luck, this first visit will be a beautiful beginning to a long friendship.

When the parents return, give them a recap. Let them know how things went. They are as eager as you are to get off on the right foot. This first visit in particular, discuss with them any incidents or behavior you found puzzling. They may be able to advise you on how to handle such matters in the future. *Always, always* report injuries or breakage even if you think you may be blamed. Chances are the mishap will be discovered anyway, and it's better to get the facts known immediately. Report all phone calls and any household occurrences you think they need to know about. Accept payment for your work (be sure it is correct) and an escort home.

33

Packing a "Goodie" Bag

Children of all ages like playthings that are new and different. If you arrive with your own bag of tricks—your "goodie" bag—you will be specially welcomed. Books, balloons, blunt scissors, paste, construction paper, a few old magazines, an inexpensive wind-up toy, a musical stuffed animal, bath crayons, goggles, pocket magnifier, or magnet are just some of the things you could include. Collect these with small effort and expense from the dimestore and possibly from your own stash of outgrown toys. You should make clear from the beginning (or there will be trouble later!) that the goodies are not gifts, but things that you share while you are there. They go home with you.

Sitting Under Special Circumstances

With Children from More Than One Family. It is not unusual for sets of parents, friends who are spending the evening out together, to want to share a sitter, particularly if the children know each other well. You might all meet in the home of one of the families, and after you and the children are settled in, the parents leave together.

This arrangement is fine, so long as you are informed ahead of time and agree to it, so long as there are no more than three children (unless you are very experienced, or it is for a short time only), and so long as you have agreed in advance on the extra pay for the extra children.

If you ever arrive at a job and unexpectedly find extra children, you will have to decide on the spot if you can handle the situation or if you'd rather not try. Whatever you decide, state your position straightforwardly, and in either case, don't

34

be embarrassed to tell the parents that in the future you would like to be asked in advance. If you do decide to take on the extra children, settle your rate before the parents leave. Very probably they intend to pay you extra, but don't assume this. How well you and the children get on will depend on how well they know each other, where they are developmentally, and, of course, how well you manage them.

With the Sick Child. Ordinarily you do not want to take care of a sick child. In the first place, it's a very big responsibility: You never know when a mild fever will shoot up dangerously high. Secondly, little sickies need the special love and assurance they can get only from their parents. Lastly, you will expose yourself—and the rest of your family—to communicable disease. But occasionally during an emergency or a time of real need you may want to help a friend.

You get a call from the mother of some children with the chicken pox ("pops"). The two older ones are getting over it, but the youngest has just come down with fever. The father is working, and no other adult is available. Since you and your sibs have already had chicken pox, you agree to care for the older two for an hour or so while the mother takes the youngest to the doctor.

In a case like this, be *doubly sure* you have a telephone number where the mother can be reached. Be sure, too, that you are well briefed before she leaves about what the children are or are not allowed to do and about what you are to do for them. If she says that they must stay in bed, keep them there with gentle persuasion—quiet games, art projects, stories, or television—no

35

rowdiness. (Bring along your goodie bag.) If she leaves medication to be given at a certain time, give it exactly then in exactly the amount she directs. *Never give a child any medication without specific instructions to do so.* Most important, if a child seems very sick after the mother leaves—feels hot, begins to vomit, complains repeatedly of discomfort—telephone her to come home immediately. Never agree to sit with a child you know to be that sick. Never sit with a sick child when you're even slightly ill yourself—the combination of germs could be awful.

In Your Own Home. Occasionally it is more convenient to care for a child in your home instead of his. Perhaps his parent is working at home or the child's room is being painted. You may need to be home to wait for a delivery or to look after your own younger sib. For the switch to work well, it must be agreeable to everyone. It serves little purpose for you to accommodate either parent—yours or the child's—if the other is inconvenienced. Also, this works only if the child is comfortable in your home. If he feels truly welcome and likes to explore new territory, he will be happy. (It's amazing how the most ordinary objects in your house will amuse him because they are unfamiliar.) If, however, he does not separate easily from his mother (see *Separation*, p. 78), or is fearful of strange surroundings, he will be better off at home.

With the Whole Family on an Outing. Once in a while you may be invited to join a family for a special event, perhaps a wedding or a short vacation. Lucky you! The parents want their children along for the occasion but are not able—or do not

36

wish—to be with them every minute. Even though this is work—you are there to take care of the children—it can be great fun. You should expect your transportation to be provided and your expenses paid. Your rate, however, becomes negotiable: It depends on how much other benefit you derive from the experience. You should not expect to be paid exorbitantly for being taken to a sumptuous vacation spot.

Overnight. When parents go away for twenty-four hours or more, they usually ask a relative to take care of the children instead of hiring a sitter. However, some parents live far away from their relatives or for other reasons cannot use them, so at some time in your career you may be asked to sit overnight. Do so only if you are very able and experienced and if you and the children know each other well. It is a tremendous responsibility and a very long haul. (You will get your first realistic view of what it is like to be a parent!)

Probably the parents will not want to pay your full hourly rate for that length of time, so be prepared to negotiate for a flat fee. On the one hand, if you are qualified to sit overnight, your rate will be high, at the top of the neighborhood range. On the other hand, despite the greater responsibility of an overnight job, the children will be asleep much of the time. Consider lowering your rate to two-thirds to three-quarters of the normal rate. Let's say, for the sake of discussion, your rate is two dollars an hour. If you will be sitting for twenty-four hours, normally that would work out to forty-eight dollars. Offer to do it for a flat thirty-six dollars. If the parents bargain you down to thirty-two, you're still doing acceptably.

You can expect the parents to provide food and

37

bedding, but you should bring everything else you need to be comfortable: clothing, toiletries, books, needlework, and so forth. You might ask a member of your family to drop in, to give you a little advice or company if needed. Do not have friends in unless you've checked it out in advance (see p. 43).

When you sit overnight, or longer, you must be prepared for every possibility. Know where the parents will be staying and how they may be reached any hour of the day. If that's not possible, have them call you at times to check in. Be even more conscientious than you usually are about writing down emergency telephone numbers, especially of neighbors and relatives who could help out in a pinch. Find out if a child has been sick recently and what you should do if there is a recurrence. Be sure everything you will need is in the house—food, formula, disposable diapers, and so forth—or that you could order an item by telephone and have it delivered. Remember that you are also house (and pet?) sitting and get instructions. Do you water plants? Walk the dog? How do you lock up at night? Who could do an emergency repair?

Some of the child care you are used to—after all, you have played with, fed, bathed, and put the children to bed before. You may not be used to getting up with them in the middle of the night or in the morning. Ask the parents what that is like and what time (!) it is apt to be. (You may decide to go to bed a little earlier than you usually do!) Explain to the children that you will be there—and their parents will be absent—for a long time. Make a book about your stay with them (see p. 151). Know in general their daily routine, their favorite activities and foods. You want a

38

balance between the familiar, so they will feel secure, and the unusual, so they will regard your being there as an adventure. Be prepared for projects, games, and outings. Keep busy. Don't give boredom or loneliness a moment to take hold, either in you or in the children, unless the children let you know they want a quiet time. At the end of your stay, you all will have gained in knowledge and experience.

Sitting Uneasily

Breaking Appointments. In babysitting, the most frequent and most annoying problem—to both parents and sitter—is cancellations. At the last minute, sometimes literally, one can call the other and break an appointment. To the parents, this means giving up an evening out—quite a disappointment—or frantically trying to find another sitter on short notice. To the sitter, this usually means a loss of money. To either, it is the annoyance of having plans for an evening scuttled. It is reasonable to expect this to happen once in a while—important things occasionally come up unexpectedly—but if it happens frequently, someone is being inconsiderate.

A particularly annoying cause of cancellations is misunderstanding. Someone wasn't clear about the date or time of a job. This is one reason to go through the trouble to keep a calendar (see p. 29). If you aren't sure whether or when you are expected, ask. Don't assume that the parent assumes.

Make very sure you are free before you accept a job; once you accept, do it. At times you might not feel like it: Maybe you were up late the night before studying for an exam; the exam itself was a killer; you had band practice after school; you've just come home—tired, hungry, and a little blue. The idea of going back out again to babysit in two hours makes you groan. *Don't cancel.* Take a shower, have a nutritious meal, and go to your job. You may not feel like a million bucks that night, but you will have kept a promise. If exams always wipe you out, next time don't schedule a babysitting job on the same day.

Once in a while in your career you will *have* to cancel. For example, early in the week you agree to babysit on Saturday night. A day or so later your parents decide to take the whole family away for the weekend. You can't sit, but you can call the parents right away—the sooner the better —to let them know. They will need time to find someone else. To make things easier, you might recommend a friend who you know is a good sitter.

You should not babysit when you are sick. What is sick? Sick is an ailment bad enough to keep you home from school or one that might be communicated to others. Small children are more susceptible to germs than older people. If in doubt (you feel fine but have the sniffles), ask the parents their preference. If you must cancel, do it as early as you can, and try to find a substitute.

If you are the one who is constantly being stood up (it's usually the same parents every time), you will have to take action. Before you do, though, be sure you have given them as much benefit of the doubt as you would want for yourself. Maybe someone has canceled out on them, or one of their children is sick. Either is reason enough for them to stay home. However, like you, they are expected to give as much notice as possible.

When last-minute cancellations happen fre-

40

quently, leaving you inconvenienced, have a talk with the parents. Explain your position to them in a straightforward way: When you accept a job with them, you make a commitment. If another parent asks you for the same time, you refuse. If the job is canceled, you have lost money. For this reason, from now on, when you accept a job with these parents, tell them you will assume a guaranteed payment for the time (perhaps a percentage of your regular rate), whether or not you actually work. That is, if they ask you for an evening, they must pay you something for it, even if they cancel. (In other businesses, this is called a cancellation fee.) This is pretty tough talk, but if you are calm and businesslike, they should accept your reasoning. If they don't, don't sit for them again.

Being Late. You shouldn't be, at least not very late and not very often. (People who are habitually late are thought by psychologists to be very angry inside. If you are always late for everything, you should think about that.) People who are ready on time are naturally annoyed to be held up by someone who isn't. Get yourself organized and out the door early enough to be at your job when you're supposed to be there. If you know you're going to be late, telephone ahead so the parents will know you're on your way.

If you arrive on time and the parents are late in leaving, it is reasonable to assume you'll be paid for the time anyway. In fact, they'll appreciate your taking over right away. If you get the children (the probable reason for their being late!) happily playing at something, the parents will be free to get dressed and out.

41

You shouldn't be angry if, once in a great while, the parents' return is delayed by traffic or by the slow service in a restaurant. But again, like you, they should be expected to telephone. When parents are habitually late, it may become unpleasant for you. Your own parents may be upset. If you have to get up early the next morning, you may be tired all day. Deal with this problem directly. Hints will do you no good.

First, try the verbal approach. Bring it up when you accept the job: "I'd be delighted to sit for you, Mrs. Kowalski, but I *must* be home by 10:30" (or 11:00, midnight, etc.). Stress the importance. You have school the next day, your parents insist (put the onus on them if you like!), whatever. If they agree to your curfew, accept the job, but remind them again before they go out: "Have a nice evening—please remember that I must be home by 10:30." If, after all this conversation, they still arrive late, you must then decide if you want to continue to babysit for them. If not, you need not bring it up when they return that evening (if you don't want to). You'll probably be tired and in no mood for that type of conversation. However, the next time they ask you to babysit, explain, without anger, why you can't: "Mr. Kowalski, I can't sit for you anymore because you always come home late. I'm tired the next day, my parents are mad at me, and it just isn't worth it." They may feel bad, but they probably won't change.

If, however, except for their lateness, you really like the people and want to continue to babysit for them, try this extremely effective approach to the problem. When it is past time for their return, and you can see that, once again, the parents will

42

be late, telephone home and ask one of your own parents (preferably your father because he will have more shock value) to come over. When he arrives, leave; let him be the one to greet the returning parents. He won't need to do much more on your behalf than to point out the time. They will be so surprised and embarrassed to see your father (or mother) that they probably will never be late again!

Being Out-of-Line. Some things you should never do on the job. Quite apart from whether these are intrinsically right or wrong, they prevent you from doing the best job.

Going to sleep: Sometimes it is *so* tempting, particularly late at night, but if you're asleep, you can't hear what's going on in the house. A thump in the next room may be a toy falling out of bed or it may be the baby. Do whatever you have to do to stay awake: Watch television; do math problems; or make yourself a cup of coffee. Best, if you know you'll be there very late, take a nap before you arrive.

Inviting friends: This is not a crime, as long as you've asked the parents ahead of time (not with your friend standing at your elbow) and as long as he or she will help, not hinder, you in baby-sitting. Sweethearts don't work out well. When you're all alone, the temptation to snuggle is overpowering. Obviously, you aren't paying much attention to anything else. Parents who walk in on you will not be charmed, no matter how liberal you may think they are.

43

Getting high: Do not take drugs or drink alcohol—ever—when you are responsible for the care and safety of another person. No matter how straight you may think you are, your perceptions are off.

There are some things that parents should never do to you:

Coming home high: This is a pain, especially if they're responsible for getting you home. Never get into a car with someone drunk or drugged. Telephone your parents to come and pick you up. Keep a low profile till they get there.

Coming on: This rarely happens, and when it does, it usually is a result of the parent's being high. Have no part of any sexual overtures. No matter how adult you may look and feel, you're still a lot younger than the parent and very vulnerable. Leave as quickly as possible. Tell your parents.

Stiffing: When a parent fails to pay you the correct amount, it almost always is a mistake or misunderstanding. Tactfully point out the error: "Didn't we agree on $1.50 an hour? I've been here three hours, so that's $4.50." Usually, this is all that's needed. However, if the parents disagree or use lack of change as an excuse for not paying you, it's best to just take what you can get and leave. Consider yourself stiffed. Never sit for them again. Warn other sitters.

By far the majority of your business transactions and conversations with parents will go smoothly, though not necessarily exactly as described in this book. People and situations differ. But given these pointers and your own common sense, you will manage well.

2. HOUSEHOLD

There is a craft to functioning well in someone else's home. It takes tact, common sense, and knowledge of how to perform a few simple household tasks. As you go about your business, keep in mind that you are in a very personal place. A home is a statement about a family's collective character, its emotional tone, intellect, interests, values, tastes, economic status, and aspirations. If you are at all observant, you can't help but take this in. Try to reserve your judgment. Accept the lifestyle for what it is. Respect the family's privacy. Treat their belongings as they would wish.

Avoiding Accidents

Your first and foremost responsibility as a babysitter is to keep the children safe. Each time you sit, make an inspection tour to locate and eliminate any potential hazards. Do this without attracting notice. A little one who sees you examining an

electrical outlet will toddle over to see what's so interesting.

Accident prevention is so important that it will be covered in almost every chapter in this book: bathroom booby traps in *Bathtime*, kitchen dangers in *Mealtime*, and so forth. All children have occasional minor accidents—bumped noses, scraped knees, and the like. Your best efforts will not prevent all of these. If worse should happen, see *First Aid/Emergencies*, pp. 153–181. Below are the more general household hazards you will need to be on the lookout for throughout the home.

Clutter underfoot can cause trips and falls. Concealed under clutter may be tiny objects like buttons, pins, and thumbtacks that can be dangerous in small hands. You don't need to clean the whole house (even if it needs it!), but do pick up questionable items and put them out of the way.

Toys should be confined to specific play areas, but in most homes they are not. Children have a way of spreading their belongings from one end of the home to another. When the situation gets out of hand, toys become dangerous clutter. Few children are very good at tidying up after themselves. They can help, but you will have to be the one to put most playthings away after use. Be aware that many toys for older children are unsafe for younger ones. Watch for small sharp parts that detach. Do not allow a child to play with an object smaller than his fist, if he is prone to put things into his mouth.

Windows, open and unscreened, invite falls. Close any unprotected window completely, or, if you must, leave it open just a little at the top. Never allow a child to climb up to a window no matter how well protected it looks. Screens and panes can loosen easily.

47

Doors should be opened and closed gently. A child might be on the other side; his fingers might be in the way. Doors leading outside or to stairways should be locked or latched.

Stairs should be completely clear of all objects at all times. When carrying a child up or down, leave one of your hands free to hold the handrail. (See illustration, p. 73.) Keep all safety gates securely fastened. If there are no safety gates, by other means block off stairways from adventurous crawlers and toddlers.

Fans can cut (sometimes completely sever) fingers. Be sure any fan is out of reach, whether it is operating or not. Never leave a child alone in a room with a fan operating.

Fireplaces are especially hazardous. Be sure the firescreen is securely in place. Never leave a child alone in a room with a fire burning.

Cigarettes are potentially lethal. They can cause serious burns themselves, and if neglected, can start larger fires. If you must smoke, do so well away from the child and, when finished, put your cigarette out with water. Never smoke while you are playing with or physically caring for a child. *Matches* and *cigarette lighters* must be kept out of the reach of all children.

Electrical outlets fascinate toddlers. Even an older child may be tempted to poke something into those two little slits that "make things go." Terrible burns and sometimes electrocution result. All unused electrical outlets should be covered with plastic safety caps. (See illustration.) Keep a watchful eye on those in use and in sight. Before *you* touch an outlet, be sure your hands are dry.

48

Cords, electrical and telephone, should be well tucked away to prevent accidental falls. Frayed

cords should not be used. Also, be aware that a
child who is teething will chew on anything; he
does not make the distinction between safe and
unsafe objects. Keep venetian blind cords, har-
nesses, leashes, and twine away from babies, who
can get these tangled around their necks.

Tools include everything from saws to staplers
to can openers. Whether or not they are safe depends on the understanding and dexterity of the
child. When in doubt about a tool, remove it as
diplomatically as possible.

Poisons lurk everywhere. You may think all
the cleaners and medicines are locked up or out of
reach, but the child may notice the bottle of nail-
polish remover on the dresser, the berries in the
dried floral arrangement. You may be surprised
that certain common houseplants—notably philo-
dendron, yew, dieffenbachia, poinsettia, African
violet, and begonia—are poisonous. You can't stop
a baby from tasting his world—it's his way of exploring—but you can remove dangerous inedibles
before he finds them. After that you still have to
monitor everything that goes into his mouth.

Finding What You Need

You have to know enough about the house's or-
ganization to find what you need to do your job.
During your first visit to the home, ask the parents
to show you where things are. Most household
items are kept in obvious places (more obvious
after you get to know the family), but different
homes are organized differently. Below is a list of
useful things which you may or may not need each
time or ever—you never know. You need not quiz
the parents the first time you visit about the where-
abouts of each of these, but you should know gen-

49

erally where to look for them. Ask the children; they may know. (Feeding, bathing, and diapering accessories are covered in other chapters.)

spare keys

clock

tool box

first-aid supplies

twine

scissors

tape

sponge or cleaning cloth

paper towels

mop

bucket

detergent

cleaner

broom

dust pan

vacuum cleaner

plumber's friend (plunger)

garbage bags

room deodorizer

tissues

writing paper

pencils, pens

light bulbs

flashlight

batteries

candles

matches

fusebox (not to touch; to show someone else)

needle and thread

thumbtacks

If you don't know where to look for something you need, it's all right to look for it in likely areas. For instance, if you need the broom, it's reasonable to look in the broom closet, pantry, or the linen closet—but not the parents' clothes closet. In general, steer clear of the parents' personal belongings, usually located in desk and dresser drawers. Such rummaging is apt to turn up business that's none of yours. This is true even if they don't put any particular areas of the home off-limits to you and the children.

50

Keeping the Place Running

When you babysit, to some extent you also house sit. Although it isn't your main responsibility, you do have to keep the place running until the parents return.

Telephone. Put all messages in writing. Don't trust your memory. Keep paper and pencil near the telephone, as well as the number where the parents can be reached.

When you answer, speak clearly and unhesitatingly: "Hello, Keller residence. No, I'm sorry. Mrs. Keller is not available now. Would you like to leave a message?" For safety reasons, unless you know the caller, do not volunteer the information that both parents are out for the evening and that you are the babysitter. If you are pressed for details, steadfastly—though politely—refuse to give them: "I don't have that information," or, "She is just not available now. If you'd like to leave your name and number, I'm sure Mrs. Keller will call you back as soon as possible."

Don't feel bad if the person seems angry. Tell the parents when they return. They will explain to their puzzled friend or relative the reason for your caution. If a caller is ever pesky or rude or threatening to you, by all means tell the parents. (See *Nuisance Call*, p. 180.)

You are not expected to take down elaborate messages, but you should jot the following: the time you received the call, which parent the call was for, the first *and* last names of the caller, whether the call is to be returned and, if so, the number. If necessary, you could also take a *brief* message. Leave your note to the parents next to

51

the telephone or some other place where they are *sure* to find it. It should read something like this:

9:30 p.m. Margaret O'Reilly called Mrs. Keller. Call her back tonight about car pool tomorrow morning. 221-6112

Printed telephone message pads, available in stationery or office supply stores, are professional-looking and handy to use. You might bring one along in your goodie bag, just for babysitting jobs.

Only in an emergency should you give out the number where the parents can be reached. Even in an emergency—unless it is impossible (because Uncle Izzy is calling from a pay telephone at the county jail, for instance)—it is better for you to take down a name and number, then telephone the parents yourself. They can come home or return the call from where they are.

It is all right for you to make an occasional personal telephone call. It is bad business, though, for you to be on at a time when the children need your attention or to be on for so long that other calls cannot get through. If you make a long-distance call, pay for it.

Visitors/Deliveries/Repairs. Ask the parents before they leave if they expect anyone to come to the house while they are away. If so, get details about who it is, why they're coming, and how you can identify them. When someone does arrive, do not open the door until you are sure he or she is the person you are expecting. Ask for identification, and check it through the window or peephole. Delivery and repair people are used to this procedure. A visitor who crabs at you for your caution is being unreasonable. Don't let the person

52

in. Tell the parents of anyone who harassed you.

Escort any delivery or repair person directly to the area of the house that concerns him. Without neglecting the children, stay close by—to keep an eye on things and to answer questions—but do not, by overfriendliness, encourage him to stay any longer than necessary. When he has finished (he may ask you to sign a receipt or voucher), escort him to the door and lock it behind him.

When groceries have been delivered, put perishables in the refrigerator. The parents will appreciate not having to come home to wilted lettuce, warm milk, and melted ice cream.

If someone arrives unexpectedly, unless you know the person, *do not open the door*, even if he or she claims to be a friend, relative, or neighbor: "I'm sorry. The Kellers are not at home right now. Please come back later." If they press: "I'm not going to open the door. I'll be glad to tell them you were here, but you'll have to come back another time." True, it is more probable that you are turning away a friend than a foe, but it is better to be cautious. Tell the parents when they return, so they can explain to the person. (An unexpected United Parcel or Parcel Post delivery is an exception, but check for the truck outside, a uniform, and/or proper identification.)

If anyone is ever truly bothersome—to the point where you're frightened—or if you think there is a prowler, call the police (see *Prowler*, p. 181).

Pets. You would be wise to ask before you accept a job what pets there are and what care, if any, they will need. Cats, birds, fish, and reptiles usually are self-sufficient most of the day. Dogs, you cannot ignore. If you don't want to be bothered with the dog, tell the parents ahead of time so

53

they can see to its care before you arrive or arrange to have it elsewhere, if only in a back room. If you are going to take care of the dog—feed it, walk it, etc.—it would be reasonable to charge a little extra though probably more politic not to. It depends how much trouble it is. Do get instructions about what it needs. Be sure to make friends with the dog before you are left alone with it and the children. You don't want it suddenly to decide that you are an intruder. Approach the dog slowly or let it come to you. Speak gently and offer your hand, palm up. When it comes to you, give it a friendly pat or a doggie treat. Never disturb a sleeping dog or one who is eating. (See *Bite, Animal or Human*, p. 158.)

Plants. The family flora need not be your concern unless you sit overnight. In that case, be sure to get specific instructions about which plants need watering, how much, and when. If a plant is knocked over and broken, clean up the dirt and crockery, but save the plant as much intact with as much soil around its roots as possible. Leave it for its owner to repot. (See *Breakage*, p. 60.)

Weather. Not that you can do anything about it, but if it changes suddenly, say, from warm to cool or from warm to hot, make the necessary adjustments to temperature controls (see p. 57), open or shut windows, and so on. If it begins to storm, bring in any toys or other belongings that may be outdoors, including laundry on the line. If the weather gets really messy—torrential rain, sleet, snow, or high winds—be prepared for the parents to be late.

54

Locks. Learn how to operate the locks on all

doors and windows, especially any double locks on entrances. (See illustration.) Ask the parents to loan you a set of keys while you're sitting. Don't forget to take them with you when you go out!

If you ever are locked out, don't panic. It isn't the end of the world. It's important that you stay calm so the children will and so you can figure out the best thing to do. Try to think what neighbor has an extra set of keys, where others might be hidden, or how you could get in without them. If you can't get back in, try telephoning the parents from a neighbor's house or a pay telephone. Unless you've had the foresight to carry it with you, the number where they can be reached will be locked up with everything else, but if you can remember exactly where they went, you might be able to look it up. If this fails, you aren't in a good spot,

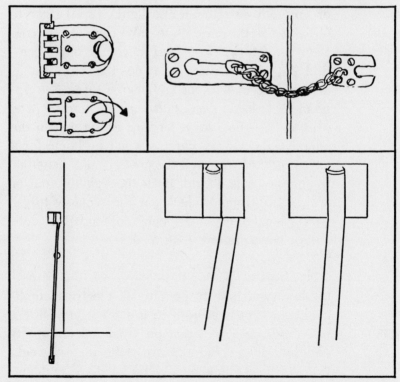

but it still isn't the end of the world. If it happens to be a nice day and the parents will be home soon, you could play with the children outdoors. If not, you could take them over to a neighbor's house or to your own. Be sure to leave a note for the parents so they'll know where you are. Be prepared for them to be a little upset.

Lights. If it's daylight when you arrive but will be dark before the parents return, ask if there are any particular lights they want turned on, especially any outside safety lights. Ask if any switches are in peculiar places—closets, pantries, in the center of a room, or around a corner. Locate spare bulbs, candles, matches, and a flashlight.

If a light goes out, replace the bulb if you can. (Be sure the switch is off.) If you don't know how or you can do without the light, it's all right to leave it for the parents to take care of. If more than one light goes out and maybe an appliance— probably as you switched it on—too many things are plugged in, and you've blown a fuse. (See *Appliances*, below.) *Do not attempt to change a fuse*, even if you know how. Unplug everything in the affected area. If the parents won't be home for a long time and you need the power, call a neighbor to come over and help. If *all* the lights go out or are greatly dimmed, look out the window to see what's happening in the neighborhood. It's probably a power failure (see p. 180).

Appliances. Before they leave, ask the parents to show you how to operate all electrical appliances that you will need to use: radio, television, hair dryer, toaster, and so on. Color television sets and high-fidelity stereos are delicate and finely tuned. Unless you know exactly what you're doing, except for *on* and *off*, don't turn knobs or push buttons.

If an appliance fails to come on, check first to see that it's plugged in and that the wall switch nearest it is in the *on* position. If you blow a fuse, see notes on *Lights*, above. *Do not attempt to replace a fuse or fix a broken appliance*, even if you know how. Wait until the parents come home, or call a neighbor for help.

Temperature Controls. Usually these will already be at the setting the family finds most comfortable, but you should know how to adjust them just in case the weather changes suddenly. Ask for directions. Don't fiddle around unless you're sure you know how, and even then don't make any radical changes. If you're uncomfortable or you think the children are, put on or take off extra clothing.

Plumbing. You assume the plumbing will behave because it usually does. Once in a while, though, something happens. Leaky faucets and pipes that drip (not *gush*) can wait for the parents, who probably already know about the problem anyway.

A backed up, overflowing toilet, however, is something you'll have to deal with. Probably, little Alexander has tried to flush his teddy bear down the toilet. First, throw absorbent materials—bath mat, towels, etc.—on the floor to soak up the water. This is especially important if you are on the second or a higher floor because the ceiling below may begin to leak. You can be sure the parents will prefer the extra laundry to replastering. Next, if you can see what's causing the problem, pull it out. (Sorry. This is no time to be fastidious.) If you

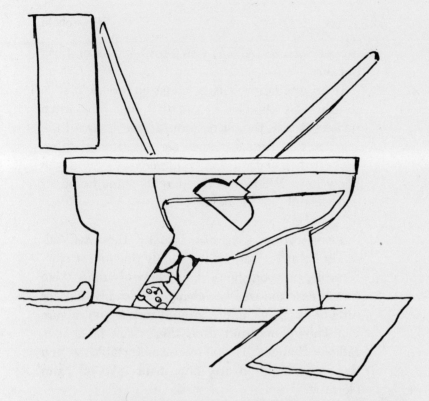

can't see the problem and there is a "plumber's friend" in the house, try using that. Put the rubber end of the plunger over the hole in the bowl of the toilet. (See illustration.) Push down hard a few times to force air through. Flush again. This may be all that's needed to dislodge whatever is causing the problem. If not, mercifully the overflow will stop soon anyway. Mop up as best you can. If you can do without the toilet for a while, wait until the parents return to tell them. If not, call them for further instructions. They may want you to call a plumber.

A real disaster—a broken pipe, for instance, flooding the bathroom or kitchen—calls for quick action. Shut the water off immediately. Turning the faucet handle will not do it. You must find the shut-off valve, usually located right under the sink (see illustration). If you can't find it, call a neigh-

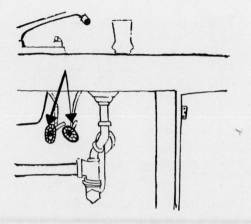

bor in quickly. When the water has been shut off, for the same reason as above, soak up what's on the floor. At this point, you should telephone the parents. They will be grateful for your resourcefulness. They may or may not be philosophic about their ruined evening.

A flood becomes extremely dangerous when the water rises high enough to come into contact with electrical wiring or when the floor begins to collapse. (See *Flood*, p. 179.)

Cleaning Up

You are not a housekeeper, so you should not concern yourself overly much with cleaning up, except after the child and, of course, yourself. At times, however, you will want or need to do more.

Special Jobs. It is perfectly all right for a parent to *ask* you to do light housework—washing dishes, vacuuming, ironing, etc. Agree to this, however, *only* if you are truly willing *and* you will be paid extra. Also, you must never allow housework to distract you from your main job of taking care of the child. He must at all times be safe and happy, or you should not do the housework. In fact, if he is young (under two years of age), plan to do it when he is asleep. If he is older and wants to help,

59

you could make it a joint project. This kind of "play" is very valuable, because it encourages a healthy attitude toward work. You must not expect much of him, though, and he will need careful supervision.

Breakage. Inevitably, sooner or later in your career, something will hit the floor and shatter. If the child is young, pick him up immediately and put him out of harm's way—in his infant seat, playpen, or highchair—even if he objects. Then clean up the breakage. If it is an appliance, *very carefully* unplug it first. If the child is old enough and wants to help, and especially if he is responsible for the breakage, ask him to hold the dustpan or garbage bag for you. Don't let him touch wiring, broken plastic, or glass. You both should be wearing shoes. If the broken object is anything that might be valued (who knows?), save the pieces in a bag for possible salvage. Be sure to sweep or vacuum thoroughly. You might want to wipe the area with a damp paper towel to pick up any treacherous slivers. *Always* report breakage to the parents, even if you dread their reaction.

Messes. Resign yourself. Children (and sometimes sitters!) make messes. Do what you have to do with a minimum of upset and no recrimination. If he is old enough, enlist the help of the child, especially if he is responsible for the mess. Don't expect him to do much.

Food and Drink. Some children, especially those just learning to feed themselves, spill at least a little of everything they put into their mouths, so it's best to give them meals and snacks in the

60

kitchen or some other place easily cleaned. Still, highchairs, cabinets, counters, and floors can become sticky with goo.

Solid foods are not too difficult to deal with. Pick up the rejects by hand or with a paper towel and put them in the garbage. Wipe over the area with a moistened sponge or paper towel. Liquids must be sopped up first with sponge or paper towels. Then, with mop or sponge, wash the area with a mild solution of detergent and water. Rinse with clear water. Be especially thorough about getting up milk or juice. Any drops you leave are sure to be stepped in and tracked around. Milk smells awful when it sours, and juice is maddeningly sticky underfoot.

If food or drink does escape the kitchen and land on the rug or furniture, get it off first with paper towel or sponge. Juice must be washed off thoroughly with plenty of clear water to prevent staining. The sooner you get to it, the better. Anything else can be washed with a mild solution of detergent and water, then rinsed with clear water, as above.

Chewing Gum. A little one discovering the joys of chewing gum is sure to take it out of his mouth so he can examine it more closely. Next thing you know, it's everywhere. Get it off his clothing, the rug or upholstery by first pulling or scraping off as much as you can by hand. Moisten a cloth or sponge with cleaner (Top Job, Mr. Clean, or the like) and dab it onto the gum that remains. When it has softened, continue pulling and scraping. (Never put any kind of cleaner or remover on varnished furniture—the gum should just rub off the wood.) If you can't get it all (that will teach

61

you to let him stuff his cheeks!), be sure to show the parents where it is so they can continue the process.

Urine. This occasionally escapes the diaper or misses the toilet. Pets have accidents, too. If only clothing or bedding is wet, just remove it and put it aside for laundering. If urine gets on the floor, wipe it up with toilet paper or paper towels. Then mop with clear water. If it's on the rug or upholstery, first blot it up with paper towels or a sponge. Then, using a cloth or a sponge, wash the area thoroughly with clear cold water. Show the parents where it was, so they can complete the clean-up if necessary. (Sometimes rugs and upholstery must be specially treated to prevent urine from staining permanently.)

Stool. Occasionally a child (or a pet) in your care will come down with diarrhea or he will just forget (see *Toileting*, p. 122). First, pick up the stool with cardboard, paper towels, or toilet paper and dispose of it in the toilet or outside garbage. If clothing or bedding is soiled, remove and rinse under hard-running hot water. Put aside for laundering. If the floor or furniture is soiled, mop or sponge the area with a mild solution of detergent and water. Rinse with clear water. If necessary, air out the room and/or use room deodorizer.

Spit-up/Vomitus. When you sit for a child under six months of age, you run an even chance of getting this on you, which is another reason you don't wear your best clothes to babysit. Even some older children vomit relatively frequently— their sensitive stomachs, acting as safety mechanisms, toss out indigestibles. For small amounts, a

62

sponge soaked in a solution of baking soda and water (about one teaspoon of soda to one cup of water) is all you need. (Be sure the soda is completely dissolved.) This will remove the smell as well as the matter. In fact, if the baby spits up frequently, you might keep a solution-dampened sponge handy in a plastic bag.

For larger amounts, as when a child suddenly becomes ill, you will first have to remove the solids. If vomitus is on clothing or bedding, remove and rinse under hard-running cold water, then soak them in a solution of baking soda and water *or* ammonia and water (about one tablespoon of soda or ammonia to one quart water). The parents will do the laundry later. If vomitus gets on the floor or furniture, first scrape it up between two pieces of cardboard. This is really the best method for removal, but if you can't find any cardboard, wipe it up with toilet paper or paper towels. Get it out of the house—flush it or throw it into the outside garbage. Then, using mop or sponge, wash the area with a solution of baking soda or ammonia and water. Rinse with clean water. Air out the room and/or use room deodorizer.

Now you know how to take care of people's houses. On to the real business of taking care of children. . . .

3.

CHILD DEVELOPMENT

To get along with any child, you need kindness, flexibility, and a sense of humor. It also helps if you know *why* he behaves as he does. The following pages will give you an overview of child development. While most "phases," or "stages," come generally under one age group or another, each child is different. Chronological age doesn't mean much. Growth periods—physical, social, and emotional—overlap. Read this chapter, yes, but also ask the child's parents to tell you what he is like. Above all, follow the leads the *child* gives you.

When you first meet a child, no matter what his age, don't overwhelm him at once with hugs and chuckles. Be friendly, but don't try to touch him. Let him keep his distance until he is sure of you. If you are relaxed, if you gradually draw him to you with questions about his likes and dislikes, his home and belongings, and especially if you bring him some small present (even if it's only a base-

ball card), he will warm up to you. Then, a gentle touch or pat will reassure him that you like him, too. All children need physical closeness. Eventually, depending on how demonstrative he is, he may greet you with bear hugs.

The way to any child's heart is through laughter and loving kindness. If he knows he can count on you for good cheer and fair-mindedness, he will forgive you almost any mistake, even giving him the wrong blanket!

Care, too, will reassure a child. To supplement the sections on safety in this chapter, read the appropriate sections in *Household*, *Mealtime*, and *Bathtime*.

BABIES

General Development

Newborns seem so small and fragile. They average at birth only twenty inches in length and a scant six to nine pounds in weight. Their digestive systems, still immature, are extremely delicate. Because their eyesight and hearing are not quite developed either, sights and sounds to them are vague, muted. Since their muscles are weak and uncoordinated, you must always support their backs and heads. Their bones are soft, and you must protect from bumps a dangerously soft spot at the top of the head (called the fontanel). Because they chill or grow too warm very quickly, you must regulate their body temperature with clothing and coverings. But they are not as helpless as they seem. What they do have going for them are good lungs and mouths that open wide. The sounds that come from those little mouths make people run to take care of them.

For the first couple of months babies spend

66

most of their time sleeping. They wake at irregular intervals for feeding, "bubbling" (or burping, to some of us), and diaper change. Then they go back to sleep. They are relatively easy to take care of as long as you keep them fed, gas-free, dry, and comfortably warm.

Slightly older babies, those who have reached the ripe age of three or four months, have gained a few pounds, so they look a little plumper. They can hold up their heads unassisted. Although you must still bubble them regularly, many of their digestive problems have disappeared and they have lost much of the newborn crankiness. Their hearing and vision have improved enough that they can begin to examine the world. Many will trade a smile for a smile.

From four to six months, muscle coordination improves even more. Lying on their tummies, most babies can lift their heads and chests. They begin to learn where their bodies end and the rest of the world begins (one reason they play with and suck their own fingers).

By six months, most can comfortably sit propped up. They begin to grasp objects and bring them to their mouths, a learning activity that continues, with refinement, for the next year or two. Between six and seven months, they can turn over; between six and eight, they can sit alone for a short time without tiring. After they can sit alone, they begin to creep, then crawl. Shortly after that, they can pull themselves up to a standing position. Some actually take a few steps unsupported by the time they are a year old.

Along with this whirlwind physical development (babies normally triple their birthweight by the end of the first year) comes social awareness. A newborn doesn't know one person from another.

In a short time, though, he becomes accustomed to the voice, the step, the particular way 'he is held, fed, and snuggled by the person who spends the most time taking care of him, usually his mother. When this person is absent and someone else cares for him, he may feel a little uncomfortable; but if the new person is relaxed and confident and is good at taking care of his needs, he is reassured.

By the time the baby is three or four months old, his personality, only hinted at before, begins to emerge. Babies, like older children and adults, are very different in the way they relate to people. Some are vocal, outgoing, and exploratory; others are more quietly observant. All babies, though, want you to pay them a lot of attention—and you should. There is no such thing as "spoiling" a baby. The more of your tender loving care and attention he gets, the better. This doesn't mean you must hover about, touching and doing every minute. That much activity would tire you both. It is enough that you take care of his needs as they arise.

Also around three or four months, with his improved vision, the baby becomes intensely interested in faces, although he still doesn't recognize individuals. When his parents are absent he may be slightly "fussier" than usual, but as long as he has no physical complaints he will accept any friendly face. Around five or six months, though, a baby begins to show a definite preference for *familiar* faces. Because he now recognizes his parents as the people who give him the most loving and most consistent care, he grows attached to them and misses them when they are absent. Around eight to ten months he will turn his face away from a stranger and may even cry. For this reason, it helps if he and his sitter have been growing used to each other over the preceding months. Eventually, as long as he has good experiences with people, the baby will become friendly again, but for the next several months he will be highly suspicious of strangers.

Along with this, he may be fearful of losing his parents, particularly his mother if, as is usual, she is the one who has nurtured him most. He may panic if she goes into the next room. Psychologists call this phase of development "separation." The baby has realized that he is separate from his mother, but he feels helpless without her, and so he is anxious. He has not yet learned that although his mother goes away sometimes, she will always come back. Wise parents will see to it that he does learn this, little by little, by going away for brief periods of time, say for only five minutes to start, then coming back when they say they will. The length of the absences can be gradually increased as the baby feels more secure.

Separation anxiety is something that we all experience from time to time as we grow up and become independent human beings. How well we are able to handle it depends, to a large degree, on how well we were helped to handle it as children, especially the first time as babies. As his sitter, you can help a baby through this first separation by making his parents' absence as pleasant as possible for him and by frequently reassuring him that they will return: "Mommy [and/or Daddy] always come[s] back." Through you, he can learn to trust people other than his parents— an important milestone on the road to independence.

Crying

All babies cry, or "fuss," some more than others, newborns more than older babies. Most of the reasons they cry don't result from your actions, so don't take the unhappiness personally. Most importantly when dealing with a crying baby, remain as calm and relaxed as possible. This is sometimes difficult with all that noise in your ear, but if you panic or become annoyed with the baby, he surely will sense your upset and cry even harder.

First, eliminate all the possibilities of physical discomfort. If necessary, systematically go through the following list:

Hunger: Small babies have a very low tolerance for hunger. The sharp pangs are so uncomfortable that they must cry. It's a survival mechanism. If they didn't cry, we wouldn't know they were hungry, and they probably wouldn't get fed as often as needed. They'd never make it! The smaller the baby, the more desperate he is to be fed, so you must be prepared ahead of time for feeding (see *Mealtime*, p. 94). It's unfair to make the baby wait while you figure out what or how much to give him.

Thirst: A baby probably will not be thirsty just after a feeding; but you might try a little water or juice (per parents' instructions) at other times, especially in hot weather.

Sleepiness: Very young babies simply conk out wherever they are. Older ones, those who are committed to discovering how the world works, may resist going to sleep for fear they will miss out on something interesting. You can tell by the fretfulness, pallor, eye-rubbing, and yawning when a little one needs a nap. You'll have to gently, but firmly, put him to bed.

70

Gas: Gas is more likely to be the problem if the baby is very young. Pick him up and, holding him in one of the bubbling positions (see illustration on p. 73), gently rub or pat his back. The gas may be a bubble left over from the last feeding or he may be about to have a bowel movement. Some babies get very cranky and gassy before elimination.

Colic: This type of stomachache gives new meaning to the word *gas*. Doctors don't understand why a few babies have colic while most don't, but they think it is hereditary and due to an immature digestive system. It has nothing to do with the baby's general health and usually disappears by the time he is three or four months old.

The symptoms are unmistakable. Shortly after a feeding and usually around the same time each day—often at night—the baby will suddenly begin crying—*really screaming*. His legs may be drawn up or stiffly stretched out. His stomach will be hard and swollen. He may cry for as much as three or four hours. It is heartbreaking and nerve-racking. You may be able to relieve his pain slightly by bubbling him over your shoulder. You may be able to distract him slightly by rocking, singing, or walking around with him. For the most part, all you can do is remain calm and comforting until it's over and he falls exhaustedly to sleep.

Most parents will not leave you with a "colicky" baby without warning. If it happens unexpectedly or you are unnerved by it, by all means telephone them to come home. It's really their job to see their baby through this bad time.

Wet or soiled diaper: Some babies can go on quite comfortably with a dirty diaper, while others find dampness unendurable. It depends on what

71

they're used to and whether or not they have diaper rash. Your nose will tell you if a baby has had a bowel movement. You can check for wetness by slipping your finger just inside the leg hole of the diaper. Follow directions for diapering on pp. 119–121, and for treating diaper rash on p. 121.

Uncomfortable clothing—too hot, too cold: Generally, a baby should have on about as many clothes, including his blanket, as you do. He should be evenly covered from neck to foot. You can tell if his body temperature is all right, first, by looking at him. If he's hot, his complexion will appear florid, and he may be perspiring a little; if cold, he'll be comparatively pale. You also can tell by feeling, not his hands and feet, which are always cool, but his neck. Slip your finger under his collar. His neck temperature is a good indicator for the rest of his body.

Uncomfortable clothing—too tight, too loose: You can sometimes comfort very tiny babies simply by wrapping them snugly in a blanket and holding them close to your body. After all, they've just emerged from the womb, a very snug, warm place. They miss it. Older babies, like anyone else, want freedom of movement. Check for tight strings or elastics and make sure the baby can wave his arms, kick, and wiggle freely.

Uncomfortable position: Some babies have very strong preferences as to how they are held or laid down to sleep. The parents probably will tip you off, but if they don't, the baby will. For holding, try the various positions illustrated on p. 73. By trial and error, you and the baby will discover the most comfortable ways to get together. For sleeping, there are fewer options. Most babies like to sleep on their tummies, so try that first.

Teething: Although this process can start any-

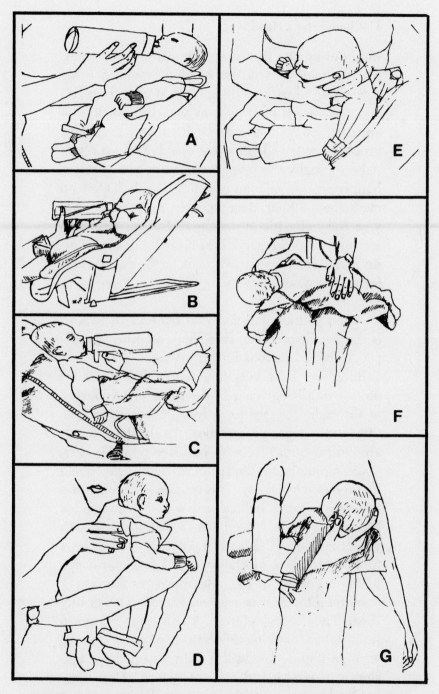

Holding a small baby: (a), (b), and (c) are good for bottle feeding; (d), (e), and (f) for "bubbling"; use (g) for going up and down stairs easily or for any time when you need one hand free.

time during the first year, the average baby gets his first tooth around six or seven months. Some babies teethe with no discomfort at all; others fret and show such symptoms as wakefulness, loss of appetite, sour stomach, slight fever, increased drooling, or swollen (even bloody) gums. Poor babes! Usually the parents will warn you if this is happening and tell you how to give relief. Give no medicine without their specific instructions. Do give the baby plenty to chew. Rubber toys and teething rings are good, best if cold. Put his favorite in the freezer compartment of the refrigerator for a little while.

When you are satisfied that none of the above is the baby's problem, there may be other, purely psychological reasons for his crying:

Boredom: Even very tiny people dislike monotony. If he's been lying in the same place looking at the same scenery for a long time (for babies, fifteen minutes is a long time), try changing things around for him. Play with him (see pp. 143–146).

Overstimulation: On the other hand, maybe he's had *too much* activity. This is different from being just sleepy. Some babies have a low tolerance for excitement. If he's been awake and playing with you or an older sib for some time, maybe he needs to be settled comfortably and left alone for a while to nod off or to contemplate his fingers.

Irritability: Babies are people, too. Things bug them. They have bad days. A baby is more apt to be irritable if he's teething, tired, or coming down with an illness. A sensitive baby can pick up tension in a family and cry about that. Also, some babies become irritable for general reasons for a period of time each day, simply expressing the frustration they feel at having to adjust to the world. This is a baby's "fussy" time. You can't do much for an irritable baby except love him. Speak softly to him. Sing a lullaby. Walk or waltz around with him. Rub his back. He'll relax eventually.

Missing his parents: This may be a problem after the baby becomes aware of the differences between people, around five or six months. Eventually, when he has learned that people other than his parents can give him good care and a good time, he will miss them less. In the meantime, you can help him by being consistently kind and careful with him, so that he will learn to trust you, and as entertaining as you know how to be—so that he will be distracted from his misery.

If the crying goes on and on, and you are unable to figure out why or to give the baby any comfort, telephone the parents. In any case, tell them about any long bouts of crying when they return. Also tell them everything you did for the baby. They may be able to tell you why he was (or still is!) crying and advise you on how to deal with the situation in the future. Don't be discouraged. As you acquire more experience with babies in general and as you get to know one in particular, you'll learn just what to do and the crying will upset you less.

Sucking

All babies need to suck, some more than others. It is one of the few "instincts" they are born with. Although sucking is necessary for nursing, it is also pleasurable and reassuring, particularly when the baby is upset, tired, teething, or coming down with an illness. Because people used to think that pacifiers and thumbsucking cause front teeth to protrude, parents once discouraged sucking by

75

bandaging a baby's thumb or putting bad-tasting deterrents on it or by taking away his pacifier. Now we know that at least before age five or six sucking has no effect on teeth. Interference with sucking causes tension in the baby, and sometimes makes him even more determined to suck. A baby —or any child—who wants to suck is telling you he is having a rough time. Certainly, you should allow him his thumb or pacifier.

"Startling"

Babies are fearful of sudden, loud noises and of falling. Even the tiniest newborn will jump, or "startle," when a balloon is burst, for instance, or his recliner collapses. He needs you to protect him from this sort of thing or comfort him if it happens.

Safety

A young baby, one who is not yet mobile, needs to be protected, first and foremost, from falls—off beds, couches, changing tables, any surface you might put him down on. Even the smallest fellow can roll off before you know it. You must always keep your eyes and at least one hand on him. The only safe places for him to be alone are his bed, carriage, playpen, and sometimes the floor, depending on whether it is clean and safe from other standpoints.

Once he begins exploring with mouth and hands, you must see that all playthings are too large to swallow, too durable to break, and have no sharp points or edges. In particular, be on the lookout for pins, buttons, beads, scissors, and other dangerous, though common, household odds and ends. Keep him away from plastic bags, cords of all types, and soft pillows. Never drink hot liquids or smoke while holding him.

76

An older sibling might unwittingly harm the baby by trying to pick the baby up, by giving him an inedible, and so forth. Never leave the two together unattended.

When the baby begins scooting around on his tummy or on hands and knees, the dangers increase. Keep him away from stairs, appliances, electrical outlets, sharp-edged furniture, or any breakables not already removed by the parents. The kitchen and bathroom are high-risk areas for burns, strangulation, poisoning, and drowning.

TODDLERS

General Development

When a baby takes his first few staggering steps, his world forever changes. No longer is he a passive observer. He is an active explorer in, what is to him, totally uncharted territory. For the next couple of years it will be his sole business to discover how everything—including himself—works. For the most part, this will be by trial-and-error.

If, for instance, as he passes through the kitchen, he takes a notion to pull the tablecloth, he doesn't realize that it and everything on it will slide onto the floor. Even if you try to explain to him what is about to happen, he will not understand—or if he does, he will not appreciate that this is not a good thing. Only if you don't make it to the table in time will he understand. Even this doesn't guarantee he won't try it again.

Taking care of a toddler keeps you on your toes. His curiosity is boundless, and as his motor coordination develops he becomes more and more venturesome—first "toddling," then walking with confidence, grasping with precision, climbing, even running and jumping. He is also learning to

77

talk, first with a few one- and two-syllable words, then in two- and three-word sentences. So he is never still, never quiet—or if he is, you'd better find out why!

A toddler is discovering, too, that he is a separate individual, and he is forming opinions about himself and his place in the world. He is learning his capabilities and his limitations. He is attempting to conform to what we consider "civilized" behavior by learning to feed himself and, eventually, to use the toilet.

Separation

The toddler continues to become an individual separate from his parents, a process he began as a baby. He needs to know that, yes, sometimes his parents go away from him, but that they always come back; that if in the meantime someone else takes care of him, he will be fine and will even have fun. If he has had generally good experiences with separation—if he has had help and understanding from his parents and sitters—he accepts new people with somewhat more confidence now.

Still, he has some fears about being left on his own with a sitter. His worst moments come, as you might imagine, just as you arrive and before his parents leave. Although he now probably realizes that they will return, he is sad that they are going. He may cry quite miserably.

It helps him to cope with his misery if, first, he is forewarned of the plans. He should not be told too far in advance, for then he will worry too much, but just before you arrive his parents should say to him: "Ronny, in a little while Mommy and Daddy are going out; Beth is coming to take care of you." This should be said lightly, pleasantly, not with a worried look and a voice of doom. It

78

also helps him if he has had that day some very high-quality "alone time" with one of his parents, preferably the one he will miss most. These are not matters that you, the sitter, have any direct control over, but if you have been having a particularly rough time with a toddler when his parents are going out the door, you might talk to them about it later and make suggestions.

Separation occurs more easily, of course, if you and the toddler know each other well. But if that isn't the case, you might try to get to know him at times other than when you are going to be sitting. If you happen to meet him and his parents on the street, by all means stop to say hello and pay him some small attention. If you can, drop by his home from time to time. The more often he sees you, even if it's only for a couple of minutes, the more accepting he will be when you arrive to babysit. If you live too far away to arrange these little meetings and visits, you might suggest to the parents that at first they leave you alone with him only for short periods of time, long enough, perhaps, to take a walk or to have a cup of coffee with a neighbor, gradually lengthening their outings as the toddler grows more secure.

Even under the best circumstances, some toddlers will always greet you with a wail and a dive for their parents' arms. This is not calculated to make everyone feel terrible, but it often has that effect. If you can be relaxed and confident at this moment, you may help everyone get through. Ask the parents to stay around a few moments, not long enough for Ronny to feel *too* powerful or for him to suspect that *they* are fearful of leaving, but long enough for the two of you to get reacquainted and for Ronny to feel a bit more secure. If you're lucky this will take only a few minutes;

79

if not, the parents may have to leave while Ronny is still unhappy. When parting finally comes, the parents should say good-bye to Ronny and resolutely go out the door. If they don't seem to know this, you can gently urge them, explaining that the parting is only made worse by being dragged out. Ronny will weather it better if he is engrossed in some activity he enjoys—especially if it is one he has shared with you many times before. Perhaps he has a favorite toy or you have brought a special treat. Whatever it is that makes him feel better, you would be wise to make it a ritual. It may not work beautifully at first—you may have to spend a long time comforting and distracting him—but eventually it will. Ronny may have a bad moment each time his parents leave, but he will learn that he also has something fun to look forward to—his time with you!

Dependence vs. Independence

A toddler still is very inexperienced. He needs a lot of help, and he knows it, but he is trying hard to grow up, to learn to do things for himself, to be his own "boss." Sometimes he gets confused about whether he wants to be dependent or independent, whether he wants to be helped or left on his own. People who take care of him get confused about this, too. One day at playtime he is unhappy unless you choose the toys for him and actually help him play. Another day he wants you only to sit on the floor in his room while he putters about by himself.

When a toddler feels dependent, he may cling, whine, or generally be fearful. When he feels independent, he is apt to be balky, contrary. He delights in his new power and exerts it by opposing you on every issue. He says "no" a hundred

80

times a day even if he doesn't mean it. Rapturous times do occur when he seems to have the two sides of his nature in balance. Joyfully he goes about his business with confidence and courage, accepting help when he knows he needs it. Many times, though, you will have to go deep within yourself to find the patience and resourcefulness to deal with him.

The rule of thumb is, whenever possible, to let him do, or try to do, as much for himself as he wants. Wait patiently, without offering help or advice, until he asks you. Encourage his efforts, congratulate his successes—in playing, eating, bathing, dressing, and so forth. Obviously, he can't do everything—he doesn't have the dexterity, and you don't have the time—but, in most instances, you can get around this tactfully.

The better part of tact is a matter of scheduling. Leave plenty of time to do things so that neither of you feels rushed. For instance, if you need to be in the park by 4:00 p.m., normally a five-minute walk, in order to get in an hour of play before dark, start the process of leaving by 3:30. Give him time to finish what he is doing. Let him try to put on his own coat. He may not be able to do this entirely by himself, but he wants to, and surely he can do some part of the job, such as pulling up the zipper after you've gotten it started. Let him decide which toy he will take. Let him walk, if he wants to, pushing his own stroller or making several side trips to collect rocks or leaves or to examine the mailbox or fire hydrant. Eventually (maybe even by 4:00!) you'll get to the park.

81

The other part of tact is attitude—yours. Perhaps it isn't really necessary that you be at the park punctually at 4:00. After all, the walk there is part of the outing and possibly an even more valuable experience, this day, than the park itself. Keep in mind that, from the attitudes of the people who care for him, the toddler is acquiring his own. He needs to feel that he can assert himself, that he has some say in what happens. He needs to know, too, that you feel he is a capable person. It is okay to try difficult things, okay to fail and try again.

If you allow a toddler his independence when he wants it, he is more apt to permit himself dependence when he needs it. He can help pull on his shoes, for example, but he needs you to tie them. Also, if he knows he can count on you for many freedoms, he is more likely to give one up occasionally. Perhaps the day you really must be in the park by 4:00 to meet his returning mother, he will be happy to plop into his stroller and be walked there quickly.

Tantrums

Life has many frustrations, and the toddler feels his deeply. No matter how careful you are to consider his feelings or to avoid conflicts with him, a time is bound to come when you have to insist that he do what he must do right then. Maybe you've been outdoors for two hours playing, the temperature is dropping, it is getting dark, and you need to go indoors to warm up and to make dinner for him. You've given him plenty of warning time and tried to persuade him with promises of food and fun at home. He won't go. If you must, pick him up and carry him home shrieking. You may feel bad about this, but he is, after all, little more than a baby and he doesn't always know what's good for him. It's time for *you* to assert yourself.

How do you deal with a full-blown temper tantrum? Many a good and competent parent has come unglued at the sight of his little one red-faced and thrashing on the floor. Your advantage is your objectivity. This is not your own flesh and blood pounding his noggin on the linoleum. You are not concerned, ultimately, with the development of his character. To you this is only an immediate, practical problem, so you are apt to stay calm as you consider what to do. It is best to put him in his bed or on the couch or some other comfortable place with his favorite blanket or stuffed animal and leave him alone a short while to get himself pulled together. Let him know you are nearby and forgiving so that, if he wants to, he can make a friendly gesture. In the meantime you might make a snack. He probably needs one. If he continues to cry and cry, maybe he wants *you* to make the friendly gesture. Give him a pat or a hug, offer a snack or a game, anything to help him save face. He's probably almost forgotten the issue that brought on his tantrum, but sometimes it helps if you can explain, in language he understands, why he had to do whatever it was he had to do: "I know you like to play outside. I like it, too, but when it is dark and we are cold and hungry, it's time for us to come in. Another day we will play outside again."

If a child is having too many tantrums—a couple each time you sit with him—he may have too many frustrations. Maybe he is chronically ill or overtired. It's time to think it over and to talk with his parents.

Exploration

A toddler's curiosity commands him. He is simply driven to learn as much about the world as his senses can absorb. He will pick up any object he encounters—from the most brilliantly conceived educational toy to a cigarette butt on the sidewalk —and sniff it, taste it, poke it with his fingers, manipulate all movable parts, shake it, hammer it, and finally drop it or toss it aside. He is not destructive (usually), just thorough in his examination.

He is also highly distractable, which is both good and bad. It's good when you need him to stop doing something, like fiddling with the gas jets on the stove. You just offer him something else equally attractive but safe to play with while you cook, such as a few spoons and plastic containers from the cupboard—then put him in his highchair where he'll be safe. His distractability is bad when you need him to do something—anything—quickly. He just can't. In the first place he isn't dexterous enough to do anything quickly and, in the second, even if he were, he goes off on too many tangents to do any task from start to finish all at once. On his way to take a bath, even if he loves his bath, he will pick up his favorite squeeze toy and chew it contemplatively for a few moments. Then he will spot his tambourine, drop the squeeze toy, and begin making music. Next the cat will catch his eye, and so forth. It takes him a long, long time to do anything or to go anywhere. Although it may seem like dawdling, it is just his relentless investigation of everything, and whenever possible, he should be allowed to do it.

You'll find the exploratory aspect of a toddler's nature easier to deal with if you can slow down to his pace and explore with him. Take the time to show him a bug in the grass or the white plume of a jet airplane. You will be helping him learn, and he will like you for it.

Aggression

About this time in his life the toddler is discovering, along with everything else, other little people. While he is not yet capable of actually playing with another child, he's certainly interested in watching or playing alongside a fellow, and depending on how aggressive he is, he may occasionally hit the other child or take away a toy —experimentally, not maliciously. If he is not aggressive, then you must protect him from those who are.

Toddlers, and even many older children, simply cannot share—toys, food, people, or space. This is natural and they should not be scolded. Neither should they be allowed to hurt each other. Simply wade into the melee, pull the parties apart, and calmly return properties to their rightful owners. If anyone is inconsolably grief-stricken (the other guy's stuff always seems better), take him aside, comfort him, and offer him something comparable.

The most frequent object of a toddler's aggression is his baby brother or sister. Depending on his nature and on how his parents handle the issue, the toddler can suffer from murderous resentment of this helpless infant. Quite apart from what he might do to the baby unintentionally, you must keep a sharp eye out for biting kisses, rib-crushing hugs, and the like. Never leave the two alone.

You can prevent some of the hostility toward the baby by not paying it too much attention at the exclusion of the toddler. Of course you must take care of the baby, who deserves as much as the toddler to be fed, bathed, changed, and snuggled. But you will make everyone happier if you find ways to include the toddler while you do these things. When you feed the baby, give the

85

toddler something to eat, too. When you hand the baby a toy, give the toddler one. When you hold the baby, ask the toddler to sit next to you while you read or tell a story. Appeal to his finer side by asking him to help you care for the baby in ways that he is able. He can find the baby's rattle, fetch a diaper, help push the carriage to the park, sing a lullaby with you.

Discipline

Like any child, a toddler must be absolutely confident that you will not permit unacceptable behavior. Since he has very few mean impulses (unless he has a younger sib he'd like to get rid of), unacceptable behavior is usually only that which is unsafe: You cannot allow him to hurt himself or anyone else. He must know that no matter how many times he attempts to clamber up into the window, you will be there to lift him down and say, "Windows are not for playing." He may not understand the danger, but he will understand your opposition. If he just wants to see outside, think of a way he can look out the window safely. Hold him in your arms, or put his highchair there and give him a snack as he watches the rain. If he wants to test you about the window, remove him far from it and distract him with play. No matter how persistently he returns to the window, no matter how he howls when you take him away, calmly and *consistently* repeat this procedure, saying, "Windows are not for playing."

Cross looks, scolding, and punishments will get you nowhere. Saying "no, no, no" a hundred times or telling him he is "bad" will only make things worse. Because a toddler is trying hard to assert his independence, these forms of discipline serve

86

only to draw the battle lines between you. They make him more determined to take you on and, in the end, undermine the relationship between you.

The only form of discipline that works is your consistent, gentle but firm, insistence that he may not commit a dangerous act. As much for his safety as for the sake of discipline, watch him. Be fast on your feet. Be there—to catch his wrist before he throws his truck into the baby's bassinette, to remove the garden shears from his reach, to catch the lamp as he pulls the cord to the edge of the table. Then distract him. Persuade him that some other activity is more fun.

Safety

The combination of his unsteadiness, his curiosity, and his total lack of judgment make the toddler a prime victim for all the terrible things that can happen to children. You need to be ever watchful—and quick—to keep him safe. Be on the lookout for dangers that only *seem* beyond his reach. Remember that he can climb now, open doors and drawers, and take things apart. His physical development is rapid. A month ago he may not have been able to clamber up on top of the refrigerator. Now, not only can he do it, he may realize that from there he can reach the contents of the cabinets above.

He still likes to taste everything, so you must continue to watch carefully everything he puts into his mouth. He won't be able to handle nuts, popcorn, balloons (unblown), or chewing gum until he's three or four.

Outdoors, he should be safe in his own fenced-in yard. Stay close to him when he's on play equipment or in the wading pool. Your hand on his arm at an unsteady moment could prevent a bad acci-

87

dent. Keep him away from garden tools, lawn mowers, toxic chemicals hiding in the garage. Do not allow him to play in driveways. When crossing streets, have him hold your hand. If he objects to this, pick him up and carry him. Do not allow him near strange dogs or cats. Even his own pet may bite or scratch when he pulls its tail (as he surely will!).

OLDER CHILDREN

General Development

By age three a child has left his babyhood behind. Most probably he speaks well enough to make himself understood by most people. (He may go through a period of "stuttering," which you should ignore. He'll get through it faster if he's given time to say what he wants to say without correction.) Because his attention span is longer and his coordination more refined, he can do a great many large and small motor tasks. He enjoys feeding and dressing himself for the most part, accepting help with the more difficult items. He has given up (if not by three, shortly after) his diaper and his bottle. He is still curious about everything and investigates everything, but his play is more organized, more imaginative. He is more sociable, more reasonable, more easily managed. The automatic balkiness of toddlerhood is gone (except for a brief resurgence when he is four). The next few years, as he approaches grade school, will be spent growing out of his complete dependence upon his parents and into his own right as an individual. His self-confidence and feelings of independence may take a big leap forward if he attends nursery school; certainly they will by the time he begins kindergarten.

Physical Growth

A child over three no longer looks like a baby, either. His legs are longer, and although he may have a little potbelly, he is no longer chubby. His muscles are developing rapidly, so he needs a lot of physical exercise. He tends to be wiggly, unable to stay in the same position for very long. He enjoys very active play—running, climbing, and especially jumping. He can handle most physical activity skillfully, if not gracefully. He tires quickly but also recovers quickly. Instead of taking naps, he prefers to "rest" by looking at a book, listening to music, or working with art materials. He uses left or right hand consistently. His first set of teeth have grown in.

Social Growth

By now, he has learned some of the basics of play with other children. He can share and take turns, if not with consistency and willingness, at least with the understanding that, over all, it is to his advantage to do so. It has occurred to him that other small people are more than just competitors for toys and adult attention. They are interesting individuals who can share his activities and his feelings the way older people cannot. He has discovered friendship! Now he not only needs but *wants* to be with other children his age regularly.

An older child is trying to learn the difference between right and wrong, and he is developing a sense of responsibility. This is sometimes difficult for him because he isn't clear about what's right or wrong, nor is he clear about his role in making things happen. He sometimes feels guilty about things he has no connection with. Perhaps, for example, he has "misbehaved" earlier in the eve-

89

ning, just before you arrive. He has dropped and broken a dinner plate. Perhaps his mother is annoyed about the accident. Shortly after, she and his father go out for the evening, leaving him at home with you. The two of you normally get on well together, but this night he feels deserted by his parents and wonders if they left him because he is "bad." Perhaps he is quiet and unhappy till bedtime, or perhaps he acts out angrily against a world that can make him feel miserable. His behavior puzzles you.

You're lucky if such a child is able to express himself well enough to tell you what happened, why he is unhappy. Then you know how to comfort him. But even if he can't tell you, you can be sure that whatever the root of the problem is, it has nothing to do with you as a person. He may test you to the limit, yes, but it's really his parents who are on his mind. This knowledge may help you keep your temper. You must be firm with him, but always friendly and forgiving.

For your part, you can avoid being the source of his bad feelings by never blaming or shaming him or *trying* to make him feel guilty. This is not to say that you should never register disapproval for something he has done or is about to do. You simply tell him, without getting angry, what he is not allowed to do and what the consequences are: "Johnny, you may not have the cookies just now. Your mom and dad said you could have them for dessert. If you eat them now, I can't give you a treat later. Please give them to me, so you may have them when it's time." If he gives them to you and you can put them out of reach until the appropriate time, good. If he runs away and eats them anyway, certainly you show disapproval and

90

explain that he is responsible: "That's too bad, Johnny. I would have liked it if you'd been able to save the cookies until after dinner." You do not heap on guilt or fear by saying anything like: "Shame on you! Your parents will be very angry when I tell them." Do give Johnny his dinner as planned. Whether he eats his meal or not, do not give him a treat afterward. If he is sad about this, explain again, without anger, the sequence of events and their consequences. Then get him interested in something else.

By the time a child is four, he does not respond well to distraction as a technique for heading off unacceptable behavior. He is quite capable of making choices and of accepting the consequences of his actions. Neither should he dwell for long on the unpleasant consequences of wrong choices. Once he's experienced them, it's time to go on to some sweeter aspect of life.

Whether or not you tell the parents of any misbehavior depends on how bad the consequences were. If anyone was hurt or if anything was broken, you must tell them. If you personally were upset by an event, you should tell them. Misdemeanors should go unmentioned.

Identification and Sex Education

One of the tasks of children is to figure out sex: What are the characteristics of males and of females and how do they behave differently? Little boys know that they will grow up to be men, little girls know they will be women. They look to the older people around them to see what this means. They learn by imitation. They copy the behaviors and attitudes of those around them who are of the same sex as they, especially their parents.

91

They also learn by asking questions, sometimes very direct questions, about genitalia and sexual matters. It is really up to the parents to see to it that a child learns about reproduction in a wholesome, unembarrassed, forthright way. But a parent may not always be around when a question is asked—maybe you will have to reply to, "How did the baby get into Mrs. O'Reilly's tummy?" or "How will it get out?" If you can have the presence of mind to calmly say something like, "Mr. O'Reilly got the baby started growing there," or "When it is time for the baby to be born, it will come out of Mrs. O'Reilly's tummy through a special place," you'll be a heroine. Anyway, you should never laugh at a child's questions or let him see your embarrassment. Just say that you don't know the answer and maybe he'd like to ask his parents when they come home.

You may notice a child handling his genitals from time to time. This may be from curiosity, tenseness, or worry. Say nothing to him about it. If he does it in public and this bothers you, simply distract him by finding an interesting toy.

Imagination

At this age a child's imagination is very vivid. Sometimes it's hard for him to tell what's real and what's unreal. He's particularly subject to wishful thinking or fantasies. For instance, he may *want* to have hit a home run so much that in telling about playing baseball he may *say* he did, when, in fact, he just tipped the ball with the bat. This is not a lie, and the story should be heard with interest and sympathy and perhaps the remark, "Boy, I'll bet you wish you could hit lots of home runs." Imaginative play should be encouraged (see p. 149) because it helps develop creativity, but if a child tells many tall tales—much of the time —it may mean he is unhappy with his life as it really is.

An active imagination leads to fears, as well as fantasies. A child can be fearful of the dark, of animals, of cripples, of death, of being hurt, or of any number of other dangers, real or imagined. It is damaging to him to have anyone make fun of his fears or to use them to manipulate him. He needs, instead, to receive extra love and reassurance that the older people around understand his fears but do not share them. Imaginative play can be useful here, too, in working through feelings.

Safety

A child this age is more surefooted and reliably obedient. He has begun to learn to take care of himself. Now is the time to help his parents teach him safety precautions, such as how to approach animals, to use tools and kitchen equipment, and to handle himself on a bicycle. Still, he may not completely understand the dangers of sharp edges, traffic, fires, and poisons. To be safe, continue to protect him from these as you would a younger child. Check on him frequently as he explores the park or immediate neighborhood. See where he is playing to be sure there are no deep holes or bodies of water, dangerous trash heaps, rickety structures, abandoned cars or refrigerators.

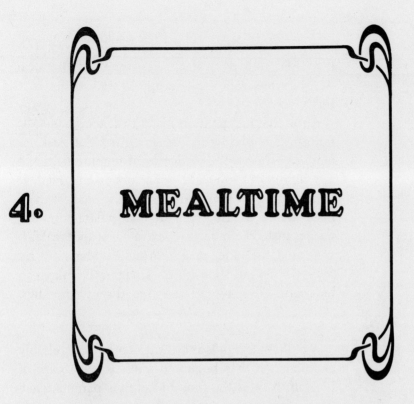

4. **MEALTIME**

Food is very important to children (as it is to us all), not just from a nutritional point of view, but psychologically as well. They learn a lot about the world from the way they are fed, and they learn a lot about the person feeding them, too. For this reason, preparing snacks and meals is one of your most important duties as a sitter.

Not that you need to be a gourmet cook. In fact, most children prefer very simple, underseasoned foods. Also, most parents will have the food prepared, or partially prepared, so that you just heat and serve.

In general, children are not adventurous eaters. Some are more accepting of new foods than others, but most prefer what they are used to. An older child, perhaps one over three, may occasionally enjoy an experiment in eating, especially if he has been allowed to help in the preparation, but

94

younger ones are more apt to be upset than challenged by a change in routine—not using a favorite bowl; giving him a banana after, not before, his meal; and so on. You are safer going exactly by parents' instructions. Let them tell you what to feed a child under three, how much, and when. Be sure you understand this before they leave. If necessary write it down.

Don't be surprised if you find different parents of same-aged children giving you very different instructions. Young children differ from each other tremendously in eating habits and food preferences. Just as you may choose to have a slice of pizza for lunch while your friend prefers a hamburger, one two-year-old may love chicken soup while another demands a frankfurter.

Children's diets vary also with their ages: Babies grow well on formula and a few soft foods; toddlers need "finger" foods that they can learn to manage themselves; and older children like a variety of tastes and textures but still can't handle heavy spices. All children are subject to their parents' and pediatricians' opinions about nutrition.

Your job is to see to it that the child receives nourishing food that he enjoys in a relaxed atmosphere. Serve him on time. Allow him to examine his food and to eat it at his own pace. Never force him to eat—not even one mouthful—more than he wants. Pay no attention to his manners. If he dawdles overlong or is obviously disinterested in eating, end the meal.

It's best to bring your own food with you or to eat at home before you come. Thoughtful people will provide a snack for you, especially if you will be in their home for many hours, but don't count on this. (Besides, you may not like what they provide!) It's usually fine to make yourself a cup of coffee or tea or to have a cold drink, but if in doubt, ask. If the parents say it's okay to have a snack without specifying what, eat moderately. Don't polish off half a ham or slice into an untouched layer cake.

Leave the kitchen at least as clean as it was: Wash and put away any dishes, pots, or pans you used; clean up any food mess made by the child; put away leftovers; throw out garbage; wipe crumbs from the counter, grease from the stove. You need not clean up after the parents unless specifically asked to do so, in which case you should be paid extra.

Keeping Them Safe

Except for the bathroom, the kitchen is the most dangerous room in the house. As you prepare his snack or meal, be sure the child is safely occupied. An older child can play quietly within your sight, well away from the cooking area. A baby or toddler should be in an infant seat, playpen, or highchair. Do not hold a child in your arms while you cook. If for some reason he is difficult to manage, you should not involve yourself with complex preparations. Stick to simple, uncooked food.

Before you even begin to do anything in the kitchen, consider the following hazards:

1. *Dangerous chemicals*, such as cleaners, bleaches, bug sprays, and the like (see other listings on p. 172), often are stored in the kitchen. Locate these and be sure they are far out of reach, preferably under lock and key. (See *Poisoning*, p. 171.)

97

2. The *stove* (see *Burns*, p. 163) is a curiosity to a small child, who recognizes that much important activity takes place around it. Use back burners only. Turn pot handles inward. If control knobs are on the front, guard against his turning them on. Be sure you understand how to operate the stove before the parents leave, especially if it has a gas oven or burners that must be lit. Some of the old models are tricky. Keep matches well out of reach.

3. *Infant seats*, *playpens*, and *highchairs*, although designed as protective equipment, can be dangerous in themselves if improperly used. Place these in a stable position well away from the stove and away from refrigerator and other doors. Do not allow a child to crawl up into a highchair unassisted. Use the safety strap, not just the tray, to keep him from slipping out. Be sure that latches on both sides of the tray are fastened.

4. Keep the child away from *electrical appliances*, especially slicers, blenders, and processors, which are particularly dangerous. Be sure you understand how to operate these. If you are unsure and can find no manual, do not attempt to use them.

5. Keep *knives* and all other sharp or pointed utensils out of the child's reach.

6. Remove *clutter* and clean *spills* underfoot at once to prevent falls.

7. *Never leave a child alone in the kitchen.*

Finding What You Need

Before the parents leave, as part of your tour of the home check out the kitchen to learn where the things are that you will need to prepare the child's snack or meal. These might be:

formula, with instructions

can opener

measuring cups, spoons

mixing bowl or pitcher

bottles, caps, nipples, and plugs

bottle brush

bottle warmer

saucepans

cooking spoons

knives

canned baby foods

warming dish

child's favorite snacks, such as crackers, dry cereal, etc.

child's eating utensils and dishes

bibs

FEEDING BABIES

Bottle-Feeding

The most important part of the diet of babies up to one year is milk or formula. They loudly demand this at fairly regular intervals. The parents will tell you at about what times you can expect the signal.

It is usual for parents of young babies, especially first babies, to be *over* prepared rather than *under* prepared for a sitter in this respect. Probably, you will go to the refrigerator and find more bottles—sterile, filled, and waiting—than you could possibly need for the length of time the parents will be away. All you will have to do is warm one and give it to the baby. Nevertheless, for the times you look in the refrigerator and find no bottle, you'd better know about their preparation. Although the following generally describes the process as it usually is performed, *many* variations exist. You should go over the parents' method with them before they leave.

99

Bottles. There are two basic types, pictured

below. The type on the left, when filled, is stored with the nipple inverted. You must unscrew the cap, remove the plug, turn the nipple right-side up, insert it into the cap, and screw the cap back onto the bottle—securely, so that it doesn't leak on the baby. The straw (center) may be used with the bottle on the left. Store the type on the right with the nipple on upright, simply covered with a large cap. It is somewhat more difficult to assemble—the plastic bag that contains the liquid must be securely attached to the rim, or it leaks—but it is better for some babies because it eliminates much swallowed air.

If you must wash a bottle for use, fill it first with hot water and dish-washing detergent. With a bottle brush, scrub the inside and rim until the bottle is free of scum and odor. Be sure the cap and nipple are equally clean. Using your thumb,

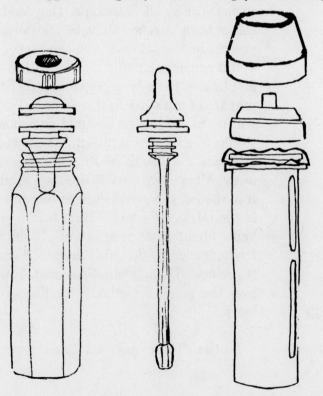

force hot water through the hole of the nipple to be sure it is clear. Ask the parents if they sterilize bottles. If so, ask them to show you their method.

Nipples. Nipples come in several shapes and sizes with different kinds of holes for different liquids. If two or more kinds of nipples are in the house, be sure you know what each is for.

Milk, Formula. Some pediatricians put babies on whole cow's milk and start weaning to the cup relatively early, but it is just as common to keep babies on formula or breast milk for at least the first year and not start, at least seriously, with a cup until later. Milk bottles are, naturally, easiest to get ready. You just pour from the container into the bottle, warm if necessary, and that's it. Formula is slightly more complicated.

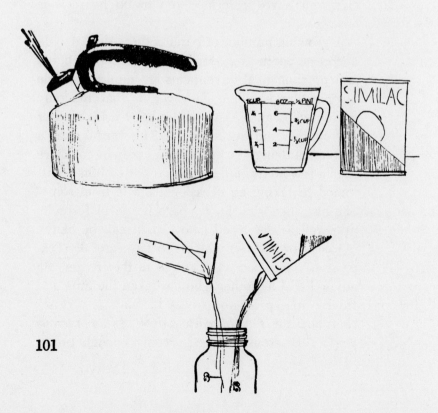

Until recently, parents often mixed formula from scratch, using a number of carefully measured ingredients, and went to great lengths to keep everything involved in the process antiseptically clean to protect the baby from germs. If the parents you are sitting for prepare formula this way, it is better that you not get involved. It's complicated and takes a lot of time. They will understand this and have bottles ready for you. Anyway, unless for some reason the baby is on a special diet, this method is rare nowadays. Most parents give their babies one of the many premixed, presterilized commercial formulas available in groceries and drugstores. Nutritionally adequate and certainly more convenient, most are a mixture of milk, water, oil, and sweetener, fortified with vitamins and minerals. Soy-based formulas are available for babies who cannot have milk. The baby's pediatrician will have prescribed the brand he feels is best.

A growing number of parents these days decide on breastfeeding for their babies. The nutritional and psychological advantages are numerous. One obvious disadvantage, however, is that the only person who can breastfeed the baby is his mother (or another nursing mother). This means that a mother can never be away from her baby for more than a few hours—*unless* she has gotten him accustomed to taking an occasional bottle from someone else, like you. It can be a bottle of formula, prepared as described below, or it can be of the mother's own milk, which she has carefully "expressed" (pumped) and stored in the freezer. Be advised that a mother who has taken the time and trouble to express and freeze her milk is very serious about it. *Do not waste a drop of this precious stuff.* Take from the freezer only enough breast

102

milk for one feeding at the time. Probably it will already be in the bottle intended for use. Do not defrost it by letting it stand on the counter, but put it under cool running water, gradually increasing the temperature, until the milk is in a liquid state. Warm the bottle for feeding as described below (p. 104). Because breast milk spoils rapidly, after the feeding is over return any milk that remains to the refrigerator.

Commercial formulas may be "ready-to-feed" or "concentrated." As it sounds, ready-to-feed is the easiest. It comes in quart-size cans, eight-ounce cans, or in little four-ounce disposable bottles. Just shake it well, and if it comes in a can, pour it into a bottle. Concentrated formula, which comes in a thirteen-ounce can, must be mixed—one part water to one part formula. (Some parents sterilize the water by boiling it. The older the baby, the less likely they are to do this, but ask.) Pour the water into a clean (sterilized?) measuring cup or pitcher, or directly into the bottle, and add an equal amount of formula. Mix. That's it.

Water. This highly underrated beverage should be offered frequently, particularly in hot weather. Ask the parents if it should be boiled (and, of course, cooled) first.

Juice. Babies' digestive systems are very sensitive, so you need to be careful about juice. Give none without being told exactly how much of what kind. Ask if it needs to be strained first, or if it needs a special nipple.

103

Warming the Bottle. Some babies, older ones, are quite used to being given bottles cold from the refrigerator, but younger ones usually need them warmed. Parents should tell you whether and how, but if you're in doubt, warm the bottle. You may find a special bottle warmer, a little thermostatic appliance that you can rely on to bring the bottle to the right temperature in the time it takes you to change a diaper. More common is the old saucepan method. Fill a pan with water, put it on a medium-hot burner, put the bottle in the water, and wait for it to heat up. This is less exact than a bottle warmer, so you must watch it and *test the temperature before you give it to the baby.* Shake the bottle and sprinkle a few drops of liquid onto your wrist. It should feel tepid or just slightly warm—not hot. If it's too hot, run cool water from the faucet over the outside of the bottle (not the nipple, if it's sterilized) until a second test tells you it's the right temperature.

Giving the Bottle. Choose a comfortable place to sit, preferably a cozy chair or the corner of a sofa with an armrest. Most babies, especially very young ones, like to be held in the crook of your left arm close to your body. Look at the positions illustrated on p. 73. You and the baby will find the one most comfortable to you both. Then, put the nipple into his mouth—he'll do the rest. Hold the bottle with your hand close to its neck. That way your fingers are close enough to touch the baby's cheek, a gesture he will find comforting.

Never prop a baby with a bottle. If you really *must* attend to another child immediately, stop the feeding temporarily.

The parents will have told you approximately how much the baby will drink, but don't be surprised if that amount is a little—a few ounces—more or less. If he seems content, you've given him the right amount. Do tell the parents how much

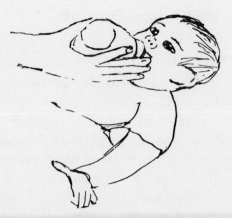

he's had in case it affects his appetite at the next feeding. Put any bottles containing leftover milk or formula back in the refrigerator. Fill empty bottles with cold water and leave them in the sink.

"Bubbling" (or Burping). It's normal for all babies to swallow some air during bottle feeding. Some are "self-burpers"; others need help getting up the air. This varies with babies' ages and digestive systems. About halfway through the feeding, some will start wiggling, spitting out the nipple. This usually means discomfort. It can also mean that the hole in the nipple is clogged. Check this. To bubble the baby, hold him in one of the positions illustrated on p. 173. Have a cloth or diaper in place to protect your own and his clothing from spit-up. Gently rub or pat his back or tummy. After the bubble comes up, offer him more from the bottle. Some babies need to be bubbled again at the end of the feeding, so give it a try. An exception would be if the baby falls asleep at the end of the feeding, as is often the case. Unless you know him to be "gassy" or "colicky" (see p. 71), don't bother with bubbling. Put him down to sleep on his tummy or right side. The bubble, if any, probably will come up by itself. Any spit-up will run out of his mouth instead of back down his throat.

Soft Foods

At some unspecific time during the first year, a baby will begin to eat a few soft foods. Some pediatricians start cereal first, others recommend fruit. Some parents prepare their babies' food(s) from scratch, others buy commercial brands. Whatever these choices, the usual routine is to give the baby one new food at the time and then to wait a week or so to see how he reacts. If he develops an allergy or for some other reason doesn't react well, the problem food is easy to identify. For this reason, *never* give a young baby anything to eat without specific instructions to do so, even if you happen to find a can of it in the pantry.

To warm baby food, spoon the amount directed into the warming dish or a saucepan. Heat to a tepid or comfortably warm temperature. Test it, as you would a bottle, on your wrist.

Some babies are in the habit of having first a little bottle, then a little soft food, and then the rest of the bottle. Others want all of one or the other first. You'll have to ask the parents. When the time comes to give him soft food, put the baby, bibbed, into his infant seat or highchair. Fasten the safety strap. (You could hold him, but this might get messy.) Using his own spoon, which probably will be small with a shallow bowl, put a small amount into his mouth. If he is just learning to eat from a spoon he may have trouble and, instead of swallowing it, push the food back out. Gently shovel it back in for another try. If he likes it, he'll eventually manage to swallow some and be willing to accept more. If he doesn't like it, fretting and squirming, he'll keep pushing it back out. In this case, forget it. He doesn't *have* to eat it, and forcing does more harm than good in the

106

long run. Even if he loves a particular food, and seems willing to eat a quart of it, don't give him more than was directed by the parents. Too much of a good thing can cause diarrhea or constipation. Go on to the next item on the menu, give him his bottle, or end the meal.

FEEDING TODDLERS

Some babies begin eating a variety of solid foods and attempt to feed themselves during the first year. In any case, the business begins in earnest for most children by the second year. At this stage, meals are easier in one sense because you are less doubtful about when, what, and how much is appropriate to feed—but they sure are messier!

A toddler goes about eating the same way he does everything else—with high spirit and a quest for information. At some time or another, he will pour, pat, pinch, squeeze, drip, or drop everything he tastes—whether or not its texture lends itself to the experiment. Be prepared for this and don't get mad. Unless he is obviously dawdling, just stand back and let him do his thing. Give yourself (and the parents) a break by always feeding him in the kitchen or some other place easily cleaned.

A toddler's appetite fluctuates surprisingly. While as a baby he'd eat just about anything you gave him because he was so hungry, now he is picky. He may go on "jags" for one type of food or another, or some days he may eat hardly anything at all. Don't worry about this. His growth rate has slowed down so he doesn't *need* to eat as much. Also, studies have shown that toddlers offered a variety of natural, nutritious foods choose a balanced diet—not on a day-to-day basis, but

107

over a period of time they will select the proteins, fats, carbohydrates, vitamins, and minerals they need to grow and do well on. (Of course, if all a child is offered are sugars and starches, he will have a deficient diet.) Wise parents make nutritious foods available and leave the choice to the child. It is best, too, to leave up to him the amount to be eaten. His body knows if it needs only a little or a lot of fuel on a given day.

Weaning to the Cup

Many toddlers still have milk, formula, or juice bottles, but by now the process of weaning to the cup has at least begun. Ask the parents how they want you to handle this. They may prefer you give the toddler his bottle(s) at specific times of the day and his cup at others (usually at meals).

Weaning can be hard on a child—he hates to give up his bottle, which by now has become an emotional support—so it usually is done very gradually. Ask the parents what they want you to do if, in their absence, he should refuse the cup and demand a bottle. Since he will be missing his parents and perhaps struggling with some pretty powerful fears (see *Separation*, p. 78), perhaps it would be wise to allow him his bottle for extra comfort. After all, he can make only so many adjustments at once.

Several kinds of children's cups on the market are designed for weaning. Some have spouts to help minimize drips, and some have rounded bottoms to minimize spills—but the child will drip and spill anyway because he wants to. Let him. Put a bib on him and put him in his highchair. Clean up when he's finished. (A child learning to drink from a cup can have great fun with it in the bathtub; see p. 136.)

Using a Spoon

When you give a toddler a soft food, such as hot cereal or applesauce, first let him have a go at it himself. If he's interested in learning how to use a spoon or if he's hungry enough, he'll make a concentrated effort, at least at first. If he gets the smallest amount on the spoon and transfers it from the bowl to his mouth before frustration sets in, he's made a major success. When it looks as if he's about to give up, you can come over with another spoon (let him keep possession of his) and lend a hand. Take care, though, that you don't *force* him to eat more than he really wants. If he stops eating after he's gotten a reasonable amount down on his own, it usually means he's had enough.

"Finger" Foods

A toddler enjoys foods he can pick up with his fingers, an activity at which he is much more successful than using a spoon. A finger food is really any that has been cut up or already comes in bite-size pieces: frankfurters, bits of chicken, carrot sticks, crackers, dry cereal, etc.

FEEDING OLDER CHILDREN

A child over three usually has given up his bottle completely, become generally adept (not flawlessly neat) at feeding himself, and developed an appreciation for a variety of tastes and textures. Except that he probably won't like heavy doses of garlic, cumin, and the like, his food preferences are much the same as an older person's. Now he wants to become involved in the actual preparation of food and in setting the table. Let him, for he really can be of help, and he needs to feel useful and trusted.

109

Cooking

You still can't allow him near a hot pot or let him use sharp utensils, but he can help with measuring, mixing, pouring, stirring, spreading, and arranging. The activity will teach him something about shared responsibility and bring the two of you closer together. Don't expect perfection. Let him see that you regard a little mess-making as part of the process. He can help clean up, too.

Setting the Table

He has given up his highchair now in favor of sitting at the table with everyone else. If his parents have not yet taught him how to set the table, this can be a project for you. As an art activity, make a placemat that's especially for him. On a

large piece of construction paper, have him draw a place setting with crayons, felt tip pens, or paints. Later at mealtime, put it at his place, so he can use it as a guide for setting. The real plate, cup, napkin, and eating utensils go right on top of the drawn ones. (See illustration.)

Notes on Nutrition

110   To maintain health and energy, everyone—children and older people alike—needs the following:

milk, including other dairy products such as cheese and yogurt; meat, poultry, or fish; eggs; green and yellow vegetables, both cooked and raw; starchy vegetables, including peanuts or peanut butter (yes, a peanut is a bean!); fruits, any or all kinds, mostly raw; whole-grain breads, crackers, cereals.

It isn't necessary to have each of these every day, but we should have most of them nearly every day and in balance over a period of time. It's best to stay away from too many starches and sugars, but a treat is fine once in a while, too.

Avoid using the promise of dessert as an incentive for finishing a meal. A child should learn to eat good food because it's enjoyable in itself, not because it will be followed by something that tastes sweeter.

Recipes

Every family has its food preferences, and usually parents will leave you specific instructions as to what to give the child and how to prepare it. Sometimes, however, particularly in selecting snacks, the choices will be left up to you and the child. Make your selections from the food groups listed above. You can find many tasty, nourishing things to eat in the pantry or refrigerator without ever having to go near the stove, but in case you feel that something hot is in order, below are a few standard favorites. Make sure they are cool enough for the child to eat. Each recipe is for one serving. All can be eaten by toddlers and older children. Check with the parents about babies.

SCRAMBLED EGG

111

Break an egg into a small bowl and beat with a fork until white and yolk are well mixed. Heat a pat (or tablespoon) of butter or margarine in a frying pan on a medium-hot burner. When the butter begins to bubble, pour in egg and cook, stirring until you reach desired consistency. Some children like runny eggs, some like them dry.

FRENCH TOAST

Break an egg into a shallow bowl that will accommodate a piece of bread lying flat. Sprinkle with a little cinnamon and beat with a fork until white and yolk are well mixed. Soak a slice of bread, on both sides, in the egg until it is absorbed. Heat a frying pan on a medium-hot burner and melt in it a pat of butter or margarine. Use a spatula to drop in the slice of bread. Fry on both sides till lightly browned.

GRILLED-CHEESE SANDWICH

Put a slice of cheese (any kind the child likes) between two slices of bread. Melt a pat of butter or margarine in a frying pan on a medium-hot burner. Use a spatula to drop in the sandwich. Fry on both sides till bread is lightly browned and cheese is melted.

If the parents have an electric broiler, grill the sandwich on medium heat.

Variation: Soak assembled sandwich in beaten egg, as you would for French toast, before frying.

HOT CEREAL (OATMEAL, FARINA, ETC.)

Prepare by package directions. When done, add one beaten egg and one teaspoon wheat germ, optional. Cook over low heat for another minute or two until egg is cooked in.

112

HAMBURGER

Take from the package of ground beef (chopped chuck or whatever) a handful of meat. Form into a smooth ball; flatten into a pattie. Heat a frying pan on a medium-hot burner. Drop in the pattie and fry on both sides to desired doneness. (Most children prefer meat done medium-well, about five minutes on each side for a smallish hamburger.) Serve plain or on toasted bun or English muffin.

Variation: Cheeseburger—During the last two minutes of cooking, place a slice of cheese on the hamburger and cover frying pan with a lid.

FRANKFURTER

Turn on the oven broiler. Place a frankfurter, whole or sliced into rounds, in a broiling pan. Cook, turning occasionally to prevent burning, about five minutes or until lightly browned. Serve plain or on toasted bun. If parents have an electric broiler, use that on medium heat.

Variation: Heat water to boiling in a small saucepan. Drop the frankfurter, whole or sliced into rounds, into the boiling water and cook for three to five minutes. (This is a little easier, but it's really better broiled.)

BAKED CHICKEN

113

Turn on oven to 350 degrees. Wash and pat dry with paper towel one or two pieces of chicken, depending on size. Place chicken in small baking dish. Brush on a tablespoon of vegetable oil or one pat of melted butter or margarine. Squeeze on juice of a quarter of a lemon (or any other citrus fruit). Sprinkle lightly with paprika (you could skip this). Bake for half an hour. Turn chicken over. Bake another half hour.

BAKED POTATO

Turn on oven to 450 degrees. Wash potato and cut out any eyes. Wrap in tin foil or place in small baking dish. Bake for one hour. Serve cut in pieces or mashed with a little butter or margarine.

NOODLES

Heat water to boiling in a small saucepan. Add a sprinkle of salt and one-half cup noodles (macaroni is best, but any will do). Cook eight to ten minutes, or time recommended by package directions. Drain. Stir in one pat of butter or margarine.

Variation: Cheese Noodles—While noodles are cooking, cut up or grate a slice (or equivalent amount) of cheese. When noodles are done and drained, stir in cheese along with butter or margarine.

STEAMED VEGETABLES

You can use any kind the child likes. Wash,

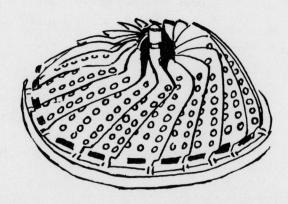

drain, peel if necessary, and cut into bite-size pieces. Heat to boiling a small amount (inch or so) of water in a sauce pan. Put in vegetable steamer (see illustration). If there isn't one, drop vegetable pieces directly into boiling water. Cook till medium-crisp, usually about eight to ten minutes. Drain. Serve with a little butter or margarine.

5.

DIAPERING/ TOILETING

From his earliest experiences with elimination, a child will form lifelong attitudes toward cleanliness and orderliness. He needs the people who care for him to change his diaper or to help him to the bathroom with cheerful acceptance, to encourage his efforts to conform to adult standards, and to congratulate his successes. He should never be made to feel that any part of his body or any product of it is disgusting or bad.

Diapering

Most children wear diapers through toddlerhood and some continue to do so, at least at night, until sometime between ages three and four. (You can see how, in a family with two children under age three, diapering can become a way of life.) Some, from earliest infancy up to the time they are toilet trained, pay no attention whatsoever to the condition of their diapers. Others can't bear to be wet

or soiled (see *Crying*, p. 70). They cry or, when a bit older, complain verbally—"My diaper needs changing!"

Each child has his own patterns of elimination. Very young babies seem to urinate constantly. It is not necessary to change immediately every slightly damp diaper. As long as the child is warm and comfortable and has no diaper rash (see p. 121), he can keep the same diaper on for a few hours. Soiled diapers should be changed as soon as possible. Young babies usually have more than one bowel movement each day, especially breast-fed babies, who may have several. They have them most often after feedings. It is also normal, however, for a baby to have only one bowel movement every couple of days. As a child gets older, he has fewer and fewer, and as his diet expands to include more and more solid foods, the color and texture changes as well. You may want to ask the parents what to expect, as surprises can be unnerving: Spectacular results have been achieved after a beet-eating binge or a blueberry popsicle!

Types of Diapers. There are two kinds, cloth and disposable. Some parents use cloth diapers because they are cheaper and, it is thought by some, if laundered correctly and changed frequently, they are less apt to promote diaper rash. They may keep several dozen on hand and launder them themselves, or they may use a diaper service, which regularly collects the dirties and delivers clean ones.

Cloth diapers must be folded to fit the baby's bottom. This usually is done as illustrated below. Get the most thickness where the most urine is apt to be. A boy needs to have the extra fold in the front; a girl needs it in the front if she lies on

118

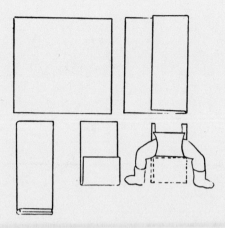

her tummy, in the back if she lies on her back. Plastic or rubber pants are sometimes put over the cloth diaper to keep the outer clothing dry.

Disposable diapers, more expensive but surely more convenient, come prefolded in various sizes, with plastic covers and adhesive tabs. There is debate over whether or not they are more apt to promote diaper rash. Many parents buy them all the time, some only for sitters or for when they take the baby on outings.

How to Diaper. First, gather within arm's reach all that you will need: a warm, soapy washcloth; another washcloth wet for rinsing; powder or lotion; a fresh diaper; pins if used; possibly fresh outer clothing.

Lay the baby on a flat surface. If this is a changing table, fasten the safety strap; otherwise keep a hand on him at all times. Even the tiniest baby can roll over before you know it. An older baby can be impossibly wiggly. Give him something fascinating to hold to keep his head and hands busy while you take care of his other end. It's a good idea, especially when you're going to change a soiled diaper, to place an absorbent pad under his bottom before you begin.

Unfasten the diaper. If it's only wet, remove

119

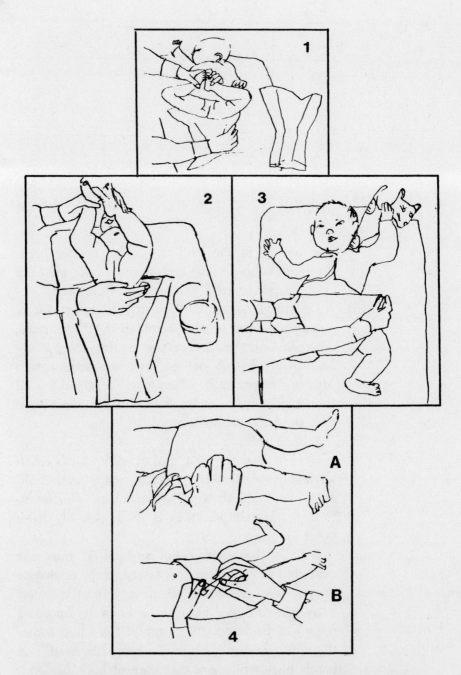

Diapering: *(1) Have fresh diaper nearby and ready to use; re-move used diaper. (2) Place back part of fresh diaper under baby's bottom; apply ointment or powder. (3) Bring front part of diaper up into position. (4) Fasten tabs (a) or pins (b). If using pins, slip your fingers under diaper's edge to protect the baby from pin prick.*

and set it aside. If it is soiled, before you pull it from under the baby, use the unsoiled front part to wipe away as much of the stool as possible. Wipe down and back toward the anus. Then lift the baby gently by the ankles and, folding the diaper in on itself, pull it from under him. Set it aside.

If the baby was only wet, you need not wash his bottom, but if he has had a bowel movement, use the warm, soapy washcloth to finish the cleaning. If the baby is a girl, take special care to clean the folds of the vagina. With the other washcloth, remove all traces of soap. (Some parents use disposable washcloths, in which case no soap is necessary.)

Again lifting the baby gently by the ankles, position a fresh diaper under his bottom. Put on powder or lotion (not both, or you'll make paste!). Fasten diaper. If using pins, be sure to place your fingers under the diaper between the pinpoint and the baby's skin; if tabs, keep powder or lotion off the adhesives, or they won't stick. If necessary, dress the baby in fresh outer clothing.

When you have made the baby comfortable and safe elsewhere, clean up the diapering area. Dispose of dirty diapers as directed by parents: Throw away disposables, first flushing any solid stool down the toilet; rinse soiled cloth diapers in the toilet, then put them in the diaper pail to soak. Put aside for laundering—perhaps in a plastic bag— soiled clothing, washcloths, or absorbent pad.

Diaper Rash. Almost all babies have some diaper rash from time to time. It's an irritation—a red, pimply rash, sometimes with pustules—caused by contact with urine and stool. If a baby is having a problem, most likely the parents will tell you and

121

give instructions for taking care of it. If you find the rash yourself, be sure to clean and dry the baby's bottom carefully. If you find an ointment in the diapering area which has specific directions for diaper rash, you can put some on. Otherwise, just use the regular powder or lotion. If the baby seems uncomfortable, telephone the parents for instructions. In any case, report the rash to them when they return. (See *Rash*, p. 174.)

Toileting

During the first year, babies are unable to control either their urine or their bowel movements. A few parents choose to try to "catch" an occasional bowel movement in the potty, but this succeeds, if at all, only as a kind of conditioning, to get the baby used to the idea. It is more usual for parents to wait until late in the second year—when the toddler has voluntarily shown some signs of readiness—to begin toilet training. It is not your job to actively participate in this process, but you should know how it's usually done, how far along the child is in learning, and how not to set back any progress that's been made.

Potty Chairs. When the child seems ready, the parents gradually introduce him to the potty. There are two types of potties, one that attaches to an adult toilet seat (left in the illustration) and one that stands alone low to the floor (right). Both have advantages. The attachable potty takes up less space in a small bathroom and gets the child accustomed to sitting on an adult toilet earlier. The separate seat is more child-size and probably less intimidating.

Experts in child development recommend that

122

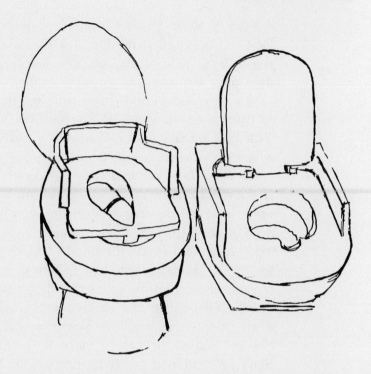

a child be allowed to sit on the potty chair fully dressed at first, to get used to it as a piece of furniture. After some time he sits on it with his diaper off. The parents or an older sib can demonstrate how they use the adult toilet. There should be no forcing, no scolding. If he wants to get up he should be allowed to do so. If he is handled gently, when he is ready, the child eventually will suceed in urinating or moving his bowels in the potty chair. From then on, with encouragement, it is a matter of time before he does so consistently. He will stay dry first during the day, then during the night as well. Eventually, without prompting, he'll perch himself unselfconsciously on the adult toilet and take care of the whole business without assistance.

123

How to Help. Discuss with the parents where the child is in toilet training. Ask how *they* want you to help. If he is younger and just beginning, they may decide to drop the issue in their absence —it isn't a question that comes up more than once or twice a day anyway. If they've been working with him for a while and he has progressed to where *he* sometimes mentions wanting to use the potty, then they will want you to help him do so. If the child is mostly trained—if he can be relied upon most of the time to use the potty—he will need little help, just an occasional reminder.

When a child comes running to you, or you can see by his dancing from foot to foot or by other obvious signs, that he needs toileting, gently but quickly take him to the bathroom. Control is difficult at this age, and the longer a child waits, the less chance he has to make it in time. But don't *force* him to go. If he refuses, let him be. You can make the idea more attractive, though, by saying something like, "Want to show me how you use your potty chair?" or "What a big person you are now to keep your diaper [or pants] dry."

Once in the bathroom, if he indicates he needs help, undo his buttons or diaper and put him on the potty. Wait with him while he urinates or moves his bowels, then help him clean himself and get his diaper or pants back on. (Usually, small boys as well as girls sit to urinate, but let him decide this.)

Encourage him, congratulate his success, but don't praise him too extravagantly or he may feel uncomfortable. Using the toilet *is* an achievement, but it should be done matter-of-factly.

124

Note: Some toddlers are fearful of a flushing toilet. You may have to wait until he is out of the bathroom and otherwise occupied before you flush away his urine or stool. Ask the parents.

Accidents. There will be many. Sometimes a child is so involved with play that he simply forgets. Sometimes a child who seemed to have been doing well with toilet training suddenly, because of some new worry or adjustment, goes back to diapers. Sometimes, too, because of illness, a child temporarily loses control of elimination. Even an older child who has been dry for a year or more occasionally wets the bed at night.

When accidents happen, there should be no upset, no recrimination. Just say, "It was an accident. Maybe next time you'll make it to the potty." Then clean him up. When reporting an accident to the child's parents, do so very tactfully or out of his hearing.

Dressing

As you change a wet or soiled diaper you will learn how to dress a wiggly child. Most of the time the parents will leave you a fresh change of clothes; if not, ask them before they leave.

First, diaper if necessary (see pp. 116–121).

Most young babies wear smocks or "stretchies" that slip on easily. Those little arms and legs aren't as fragile as they look. They won't snap when bent! Just be gentle, especially with fingers and toes, and whenever pulling a garment over the head, make sure the neck opening is large enough that you don't have to yank it over his face and ears. Most babies hate this.

125

An older baby or toddler may be very wiggly. You'll have to distract him with a toy. Or he may want to attempt to dress himself. This will take patience on your part. Lay the clothing out so he can see where to put which limbs, and help him a little by putting the things on partway for him. If he sees that you're willing to let him try, he may feel more cooperative.

An older child will need the barest assistance. Help him find what he needs and lend a hand only when asked or obviously needed.

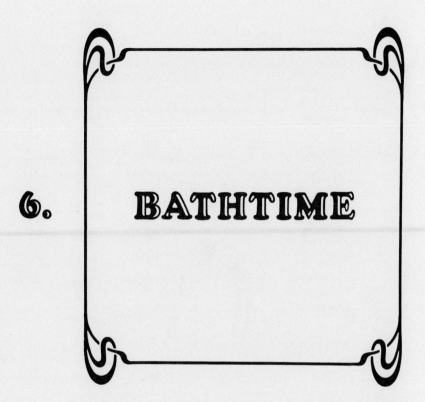

6. **BATHTIME**

Usually the parents will tell you if they want you to give the child a bath, and usually, if they do, it's more for the sake of his routine than for cleanliness. Bathtime is funtime for your friend—it's a great opportunity for creative play, and it can be just the thing to help him relax, to wind down before bed. He won't argue about it if you suggest it the right way: "Do you like to play with bubbles?" "Let's try this boat in the bathtub." "After your bath, we can have a snack and a story." As always, ask the parents how and when they give the bath, and follow their example. (See also *Dressing*, p. 125.)

Remember that the bathroom is one of the two most dangerous rooms in the house. (The other is the kitchen.) Here are some precautions you must always take.

127

Keeping Them Safe

1. Check first to be sure that no medicines, toiletries, cosmetics, cleaners, scissors, or appliances are left about. Move any *well* out of the child's reach.

2. Fill the tub no more than a few inches deep, depending on the age and size of the child. No child needs a tub full to the brim.

3. *Always* check the temperature of the bath water with your elbow or wrist just before you put the child in. (Sometimes hot water gets hotter as it runs.) It should feel just tepid for babies, a little warmer for older children.

4. Turn taps and shower control off *hard*—too hard for the child to turn back on.

5. Be sure that you have everything you will need—soap, washcloth, bath toys, towel—within easy reach before you put the child into the tub.

6. Look to see if there is some nonskid material in the tub to prevent falls. If nothing else, have the child sit on a towel. Put a bathmat or towel on the floor beside the tub.

7. Lift a small child into the tub by placing your hands under his arms. Feet always touch the water first. Lift him out the same way. Never allow a child to step in or out on the rim of the tub.

8. Never attempt to dry a child's hair with an electric dryer while he is in the tub.

9. Never, *never*, leave a child alone in the bathroom—not to answer the door, to answer the telephone, to get a towel or anything else. If you have other children to care for, have them safely occupied before you begin or have them in the bathroom with you.

GETTING BABIES CLEAN

Most parents will not ask you to bathe a very young baby. There is just too much risk of difficulty and even accident. Unless you have often bathed your own baby brother or sister, you shouldn't try to do it. Tell the parents you don't have enough experience and ask them not to give you that responsibility until the baby is older. You might offer to help them bathe the baby before they leave or make arrangements to visit (free of charge) one day when everyone has more time for a lesson. However, if you do have experience and both you and the parents feel confident of your ability, go ahead.

Ask the parents what time they usually bathe the baby. Probably they will want you to do it before you feed him—unless he is too hungry to wait—because he'll want to sleep after he eats.

Ask them, too, where he is bathed. Small babies, those who cannot sit alone, usually are bathed on a waist-high surface—in a bathinette, a sink, or a small tub on a table. But if the baby can sit alone, he can be put in an inch or so of tepid water in the family tub.

When it is time to begin, first think the process through. Put the baby down in a safe place while you get ready. Get together within arm's reach everything you will need: washcloth, soap, towel, lotion or powder, diaper, pins if used, and clothing. Get the water the right level and temperature. Then, undress the baby.

Holding him securely—with one arm (your left if you're right-handed, your right if you're left-handed) supporting his head and shoulders, the other supporting his back and buttocks—slowly and gently lower him into the water, feet first.

130

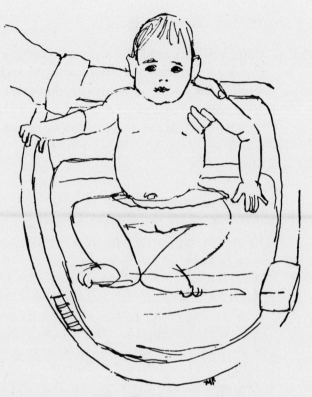

(See illustration.) Don't just plop him in. He needs time to get used to it. If he can't sit alone, continue to support his head and shoulders with one arm. If he can, he doesn't need so much support, but you must still keep a hand on him in case he loses his balance.

With your free hand, soap him lightly. Then rinse away the soap thoroughly, particularly in the folds of skin where he has baby fat, so he won't get chafed there. Don't put soap or even very much water on his face or head; just wipe gently with a warm, well wrung-out washcloth.

When you have both had enough of the bath, lift him out—again holding him securely—and place him on his dressing surface. (You must *always* keep one hand on the baby in case he turns over. Even tiny babies can flip right off a bed or table before you know it, so you should have everything you will need within reach before you start.) Cover him immediately with a towel and dry him well, so he won't get cold. Pat, don't rub, and pay attention to folds of skin.

Now you can put baby lotion or powder on him (not both—they'll make paste). Diaper and dress him.

Sponge Bath. Babies usually don't get very dirty, so if—for whatever reason—you don't want to give a tub bath, you can always give him a sponge bath.

Gather all you will need: pan of warm water, washcloth, soap, towel, lotion or powder, diaper, pins if used, clothing. Put all these things on your surface or within easy reach. Then undress the baby and cover him with a towel, so he'll stay warm.

With a warm, well wrung-out washcloth, gently wipe his face clean. Using soap if you wish, go on to other areas of his body, soaping and rinsing each before you go on to the next. Be sure to wipe off all traces of soap, especially from folds of skin. If you don't want to sponge-bathe him completely, just do his face and diaper area. Dry, diaper, and dress him.

Later, when the baby is snoozing or playing peacefully, you can put away the bath things and tidy up.

Sponge Bath for Fever. If a child becomes hot with fever while in your care (see *With the Sick Child*, p. 35, and *Fever*, p. 169), *after* you have telephoned the parents to come home, you can give him a sponge bath to help bring the fever down. He will be feeling too ill to be moved

132

around much, so this is best done as he lies in his own bed. Do as described above, but use no soap.

GETTING TODDLERS CLEAN

At this stage, baths are much easier, but you still must be very careful to prevent accidents. Children this age are active and curious but lacking in judgment and self-control, and this is as much true of them in the bathtub as anywhere else. You must always have a hand on him to prevent a slip or to move exploring fingers away from the hot-water tap. You must think of ways to make bathing fun, so he'll want to do it. And you must be resigned to getting wet!

Things tend to go smoother if the parents have told the child that you will give him a bath, but in any case give him fair warning before you begin. He may be all for it, but he will want to finish what he is doing first.

Be warned that there is an age, usually between one and two, when fears about the bath are very common. Your friend may have fallen in the tub and been hurt or gotten soap in his eyes, or he may be afraid of going down the drain with the bath water (yes!). If the parents warn you of this or the child seems afraid, skip it. A bath isn't that important. If he's dirty, you can just give him a sponge bath.

Once the two of you have agreed that a tub bath is a fine idea, go ahead. You can let him help you get ready. He can find his favorite bath toy, maybe pull off his own socks, while you are locating other things and getting the water ready.

133

Once he's in the bath, he'll be ready to play, and while you're playing with him, you can—mat-

ter-of-factly and without fanfare—soap and rinse
a little here and there. It probably will not be a
good idea to put soap on his face. He may not even
like your wiping his face, so do it quickly and
gently.

When you're both finished, lift him out, pat him
dry, and get him dressed. Later, you can drain the
bath water and clean up. You probably will need
to mop!

Washing Hair. This is a tricky business and
better left to the parents, but if you *must* do it
(he has a headful of maple syrup, or some awful
thing), first try wiping it out with a very wet washcloth. That failing, try this.

Have the water no more than an inch deep. Persuade him gently to lie down flat in the water rest-
ing his head either on your hand or on the bottom
of the tub. Tell him a story about the cracks in
the ceiling. Maybe there's something interesting
about the showerhead or the wallpaper he can
look at. The water should not come up over his
ears.

If at this point all is well, using your hand, the
sponge, or washcloth, wet his hair. Take care that
the water runs from his hairline to the back of his
head. Quickly and gently and with a small amount
of "baby" shampoo, wash the goo out of his hair.
Rinse carefully, keeping the shampoo well away
from his eyes. When you're finished, help him sit
up so that the water runs to the back of his head.

Another solution to the trauma of hair-washing
is a pair of goggles. With his eyes protected, he
will allow you to wash and rinse as necessary—
if he isn't afraid of the goggles. This might be a
useful item for your goodie bag.

134

No technique will work with a child who is skittish about the bath to begin with. Forget it. Better he greet his parents with sticky hair than hysteria.

Once he's out of the tub, dry his hair with a towel or, if he isn't afraid, with an electric dryer on low temperature.

Brushing Teeth. He may love this. Ask his parents. The object is not so much to get his few teeth clean as to get him in the habit of regular brushing. He probably has his own toothbrush, which he will chew, dribbling toothpaste everywhere. You can have a great time teaching him how to spit!

Trimming Nails. Don't try it. He's too wiggly. Tell his parents about any really wicked ones.

GETTING OLDER CHILDREN CLEAN

By this age, a child can reasonably be expected to bathe himself, at least partially. Your little friend may be feeling so independent that he may even demand that you leave the bathroom. Don't do it! Tell him you're lonely or that you want to play with him. If you must, sit just outside the door—but be ready to move quickly to prevent an accident or to offer assistance.

Washing hair and trimming nails are much easier now. He can keep still longer (well, a *little* longer) and follow a few instructions. He probably can brush his teeth very well without help. Clean-up, as always, is yours, although he can be expected to help fold his towel or put his dirty clothes in the laundry hamper.

LETTING BABIES PLAY

A very young baby needs no special water play. Simply being in the water—feeling it on his skin, hearing it gurgle and splash as you bathe him—is stimulation enough. Even an older baby, one who can sit alone, doesn't need much in the way of bath toys. In fact, too many brightly colored objects floating in the water can distract and confuse him. All he needs is his sponge, a plastic block, or a squeeze toy. These he can grasp easily, bat around, and suck and chew to his heart's content. The water itself is his best plaything.

LETTING TODDLERS PLAY

A child this age thoroughly enjoys playing in water (so long as he isn't afraid of it). He still likes his sponge and other floating toys but now also enjoys simple games and more active splashing.

The kitchen is a good source of bath toys. You can give him a few plastic containers of different shapes and sizes, a basting brush to "paint" with, or a squirt bottle—not too many things at once. If he has a special cup he's learning to drink from, you can give it to him while he's in the bathtub. There he can practice spilling all he likes. (No soap in the water at this time!)

Now that he can stand, he loves to wade around, and even more, he loves to make a big splash. Holding his hand, you can help him slide down the end of the tub. This is very daring to him, and as long as he feels safe, it's a good game. It helps him learn that the water is friendly and fun, even when it splashes on his face. A small amount of bubbles—either the commercial kind or homemade

136

with soap flakes—can be introduced at this age. Remember to keep the water shallow.

LETTING OLDER CHILDREN PLAY

When a child is old enough to understand how to blow, not suck, he can have wonderful fun with bubble pipes and soda straws. You can make spectacular bubbles by adding a few drops of vegetable coloring to the water. If you happen to have a few bath crayons in your bag of tricks, your friend will love you for them.

With his newly acquired imagination, ordinary toys—even the old ones he's tired of—take on new interest in the bathtub. (Be sure they're waterproof! If in doubt about one, help him select something else.)

Children this age like to feel useful, too. Let him wash out an article or two of the dirty clothing he's just taken off, and by all means let him help you wash out the tub when he's finished.

137

7. BEDTIME

Most children go off to bed easily. They're tired, and if handled with tact and attention to their physical and psychological comfort, they fall asleep gratefully. Some children, though, fight to the finish. This varies from household to household, depending on the ages of the children, their personalities, and the precedents set by parents. You can't change any of the above factors, but you can make bedtime as easy as possible by, first, discussing with the parents details of the usual routine and their strategies when the children resist sleep. Next, set some precedents of your own. A child needs to know that he can count on you for reassurance, but he also needs to know that, for all your kindness and understanding, you won't take any baloney.

BABIES

138   Though the hours may be irregular, a very young baby sleeps much of the time. Usually, with

full tummy, dry diaper, and warm blanket he goes right to sleep. He may drop off in your arms close to the end of a feeding, especially if you rock him. Put him down in his usual place—bassinette, cradle, or crib. Unless his parents have told you he prefers his back, place him on his tummy or right side. Cover him appropriately for the room temperature—about as you would yourself—and tiptoe out. He needs no pillow. Leave a dim light on nearby so you can check on him frequently. He may grunt, gurgle, whimper, or burp in his sleep, but don't let this bother you. Unless he actually wakes and cries, leave him alone. An older baby, say one over four or five months, may already have formed some opinions about what bedtime should be like. He may already have a favorite blanket or direction he likes to face.

If the baby does wake up after he supposedly is out for the evening, give him a few minutes—five to ten—to try to fuss himself back to sleep. If he stays awake, see if you can soothe him back by walking or rocking him. Perhaps his only problem is a bubble left over from his last feeding. If this is the case, after the bubble comes up, you could offer him a little more from his bottle. If he continues to cry, check through the list of possible reasons on pp. 70–75. It's possible you will have to keep him in your arms until his parents return.

TODDLERS

A toddler's sleep pattern is more regular than a baby's—he needs about twelve hours at night and one longish nap during the day—but at this age separation anxiety (see p. 78) can interfere with his going to sleep when he's supposed to. Bedtime can get a little tricky.

140

Try to keep him distracted from any unhappiness by playing with him with his favorite toys or perhaps with an unfamiliar one from your goodie bag. Stick close to his routine. If this includes a bath, make it a long one with lots of water play. Before actual bedtime, give him plenty of notice and "winding-down" time—quiet play, a story (not a scary one), or a snack. You could spend some time with him putting away the toys in his room. When it's time for bed be sure to remember which is the right blanket, the right stuffed animal, the right lullaby. Does he use a night light? Take a bottle to bed with him? When he's finally in, tuck him in affectionately, put the sides of the crib in their highest position, and go out.

If you're lucky, this will be it. But it may be that the absence of his parents will be just too much to bear alone in the darkened room. You may have to go back in and give him extra cuddling. Perhaps if you just sit quietly with him he will drop off, or if he is used to rocking, he will go to sleep in your arms. If none of this works, let him up for another hour of *quiet* play. You could try putting him on the couch with blanket and pillow while you sit nearby reading or watching television. He may go to sleep there, or he may get drowsy enough that you could put him back to bed. You hope that he won't still be there, wide-eyed, when his parents come home, but if he is, you should discuss with them what to do about the problem in the future. One solution would be for them to put their toddler to sleep before they go out.

OLDER CHILDREN

141

Because of the development of their very vivid imaginations, children who are three, four, and five years old are susceptible to a variety of fears (see p. 93). These can keep them from dropping off to sleep or wake them up later in the form of nightmares. Give a child this age the same "winding-down" and extra cuddling you would give a toddler. Before tucking him in, sit with him a long time on the bed playing quietly or reading *two* stories. If he expresses some fear, let him know you understand, but you're absolutely sure that there's no monster in the closet. The two of you can take a look to be sure. Let him know that you are going to be right in the next room—he'll be able to hear you humming or washing dishes or whatever. If he still seems genuinely fearful and wants you to stay with him, do so, but don't allow yourself to be engaged in further conversation. Your presence should be enough: "We've talked a lot—now it's time to go to sleep."

If a child wakens with a nightmare, go in to him immediately. Don't expect him to be rational about the dream or able to separate it from reality. Just cuddle and reassure him. You may have to sit quietly in the room until he drops off to sleep.

Much older children, those over six, know pretty well what is real and what is imaginary. Any attempts on their part to delay bedtime should be dealt with patiently but firmly. Set a limit (once or twice) to the number of times you'll bring a glass of water or allow them up to go to the bathroom.

8. PLAYTIME

To be a good sitter you must be businesslike and orderly and know how to take care of children's physical needs: feeding, bathing, diapering or toileting, and putting them to bed. But if you know how to do these things *and* you know how to *play*—you're an ace. Not only will the parents value you for your competence, the children will delight in the fun you give them and look forward to your arrival.

BABIES

Newborn babies are not awake much of the time nor are they much aware of the world and people around them. All they really need from you is to have their physical needs met and plenty of holding and cuddling. It's not until they're several weeks old that you can begin to play with them a bit. Even then, at first they can take only a

143

couple of minutes of play at a time before they tire. They have a very short attention span, and too much play makes them upset. At the first sign of unwillingness—they turn their eyes or faces away or whimper a little—stop the play. Snuggle and reassure them.

Up to and around three months of age, a baby likes "gurgling" games. You can communicate with him by imitating the sounds he makes. When you hear him making little noises to himself, put your face where he can see it and try your best to make exactly the same sound he does. Do this softly and with a smiling face. Each time he makes a sound, you make the sound. He will look at you with interest and may even reward you with a smile. In general, he likes your face. Try making funny ones.

He likes looking at other things, too, especially mobiles. If he has one hanging over his crib or playpen, that's good, but you can make him new ones all the time. All you need is ribbon or string with one or two shiny or brightly colored objects attached—a spoon, a cup, your bracelet, whatever. He can't really grab yet, so these are just for looking.

He likes lights. In a semidarkened room, turn on a flashlight or a dim lamp and turn him toward it.

He has discovered fingers, his and yours. Let him suck his own, play a gentle tug-of-war with yours. (Wash your hands first, as he may succeed in getting yours into his mouth, too.)

He might like tickling—very gentle—on the chin, cheek, tummy, or whatever part invites you. Some don't like it, though, so at the first sign of distress, stop and reassure him.

He likes to be held and walked around. The

145

changing scenery stimulates him. Take him over to the window, the clock on the mantel, or a brightly colored picture on the wall.

He enjoys music, so for a change of pace put on the radio or record player and dance with him. Not too lively, although some babies do like to boogie. If he's tired or fretful, a romantic slow dance might soothe him to sleep.

Sing with the music—or just on your own if you feel like it. He doesn't know whether you're on key; he just likes the sound of your voice.

After three months, a baby's play becomes a bit more active. He can sit propped up and make swiping grabs at things. He likes to gum his pacifier or the nipple of his bottle. If he's taking solid food, he'll touch it with his fingers, smear it around his mouth.

He still finds faces interesting, doll, human, or picture—including his own in a mirror—and especially if they're smiling.

If you support him well, he likes a little gentle knee-bouncing.

"Pat-a-cake" is good.

By six months he can laugh aloud with you. You can do "peek-a-boo": Disappear briefly, duck down or around the corner from his vision—then pop back in. "Peek-a-boo!" Always with smiling face. The more he laughs, the more exuberant you can become, but you must always gradually calm back down to a more relaxed pace.

Another good game is "give-and-take." You give the baby a rattle or some other object he can hold easily. You take it back. You hold it out, and he takes it from you. And so forth, with exclamations.

Try crumpling pieces of paper, the noisier the better, then throwing them at the baby. He will scoop them up, bat them about, and laugh.

146

Toward the end of the first year, the baby becomes less interested in what you're doing and more interested in discovering what he can do, whether this is crawling, pulling up to a standing position, or actually taking a step or two.

He begins to taste-test in earnest everything he finds, playing and learning at the same time. In his travels he bangs, pokes, twists, turns, pushes, and pulls all that he encounters. He discovers how to crawl in, out, and under boxes, chairs, and tables. From his highchair, stroller, or carriage, he experiments with dropping—toys, food, utensils, articles of clothing. Since he doesn't really understand where these items go or how to get them back, you will have to retrieve them. If the parents haven't already done so, you could tie the toys onto the equipment with ribbons or string.

(See also *Bathtime*, p. 136.)

TODDLERS

Now the "baby" is really out and about and into everything. His parents have probably child-proofed the home so you don't have to say constantly, "no, no," or, "don't touch." Put any unsafe or unsturdy object you spy out of his reach.

You can play "chase" with him, but he will have to be the one to chase you. He won't understand running away until he is older. Get down on all fours and scramble around with him. He'll think you're a riot. While you're being chased you can let him see you hide behind a chair. Finding you will be the best fun yet.

You also can hide objects, but a younger toddler won't be able to find them unless he sees where you put them.

One of his best entertainments this year will be

147

emptying and filling containers. At first he will prefer emptying—large (unswallowable) beads from boxes, flatware from the dishwasher onto the floor, clothing from his chest-of-drawers. Closer to two, it will occur to him to put things back.

You can start him on simplified ball playing. Sit on the floor and roll a large ball, none too exactly, back and forth to each other.

About now he will discover music. No longer a background noise, it will be something to listen to intently. Many children like to bang an instrument (a real one, pot, or pot cover) or dance or march around to the music. As he is in the act of marching, you can suggest "follow-the-leader" and explore the entire home. Still banging instruments, proceed to the yard or park.

A great game to play is "pretend birthday." This works best, of course, if he has had some experience with birthday parties. You can invite all his dolls and stuffed animals. Wrap up one of his old toys in paper (let him see you do this), devise a pretend cake (out of something as simple as a piece of bread), and sing "Happy Birthday," blowing out the pretend candles.

An older toddler, getting closer to three years of age, can really get into this kind of pretense. He can pretend almost any regular or not-so-regular event in his life, such as a trip to the grocery store, which gives him an opportunity to remember and name the foods he has seen his parents buy, or to the pediatrician, which perhaps will help him work through some of his fears about those visits. All such pretend games are more successful if you participate fully and especially if you occasionally change roles with him—sometimes you are the grocer and he the customer, and vice versa.

148

His parents probably have introduced him to books some time earlier, but now you can really enjoy them with him. He has a hard time following the plot of a story, but nursery rhymes are fine and also picture books, if the pictures are of objects he recognizes.

Among the toys a toddler most likes are dolls, bean bags, large balls, blocks, books, water paints (only one or two colors at a time), clay or dough, crayons, two- or three-part puzzles, and cuddly toy animals (one of which may have the high honor of being his "lovie" or "comforter").

He definitely loves water play involving various-sized containers, bubbles, pipes, and straws. (See *Bathtime*, p. 136.)

Outdoors, he wants to run, walk, and jump. It's fun to balance on walls while holding your hand. Let him wander away from you a short way to explore—this is good for his developing feeling of independence—but don't let him get out of sight, and be quick to retrieve him.

The best playground equipment for him is swings (the kind with backs and safety straps), slides (watch him up the steps, catch him at the bottom), and the sandbox, for which he will need digging toys.

OLDER CHILDREN

Since children over three are highly mobile and well-coordinated and since by now (with help) their imaginations have developed, their play becomes highly complex. They also are quite capable of suggesting activities to you and often want to include their friends. Allow this whenever possible.

149

Much of their play centers around what they

consider "real" play. They like to imitate adult activities or professional occupations: doctor, fireman, grocery store, schoolroom, policeman, etc. Often they need each other, and especially you, to participate to make the play more lifelike. The drama of these games can be varied and entertaining just to watch.

A very valuable type of this kind of play is "houseplay." This involves a pretend family with various roles and rotating assignments. It's best when a child actually participates in household chores, such as putting away toys, sweeping, dusting, vacuuming, and taking out the trash. Not only is he able to give real help, he is developing lifelong attitudes toward family roles and household responsibilities. If he has been a contributor to whatever mess you are cleaning, so much the better.

Children this age need, also, to channel their physical aggressions into acceptable forms. If, indoors, you can see by his boisterous, trying behavior that a child needs to get rid of some angry impulses, you can play "kick the pillow." Hold the pillow yourself or prop it against a soft piece of furniture. Have him kick and punch the pillow (a stuffed animal works just as well) with all his force until he tires of it. It may save his sibs some lumps!

Creative materials for a child this age can be a bit more out of the ordinary than the usual paint, crayons, clay, and paste. Scotch tape, paper clips, pipe cleaners, staplers, and hole punches make interesting toys.

He can usually handle puzzles of ten pieces or more.

150

Books he enjoys have stories about people, feelings, events, and occupations that he recognizes.

He likes to turn pages and to touch illustrations as you read.

He likes sorting things—putting pairs of socks together, flatware into the appropriate trays, blocks into their containers, parts of toys and games into their proper boxes.

Some good indoor toys for him include smaller, more intricate, interlocking building blocks; trains, trucks, and cars with miniature people in them; tools for hammering, screwing, and sawing (with your supervision); dolls, now with wardrobes; dress-up clothes, especially hats and capes; flashcards with pictures of ABCs and animals; a chalkboard; a pocket magnifying glass; or magnets.

Now the choices children make may reflect sexual identification: Boys may choose to play pirates, girls to play nurses. Accept and encourage any reversal of these roles.

Something you can do together is *make* a book: Put a few sheets of paper (not more than two to four) together and fold in half to make a booklet. With crayons or colored pencils, tell a story in pictures, preferably a "true" story from the child's experience. For instance, if you have just that day taken a walk outdoors with him, draw pictures and tell the story of the walk. Making a book is particularly helpful not just as an entertainment, but as an aid when the child is having some sort of difficult adjustment. For instance, if the parents will be away for a longer-than-usual period of time—overnight or for the whole weekend—you can help the child handle the situation by telling the "story." Seeing it in pictures—the parents' leaving, his experiences with you while they are away, and their return—will help him understand and perhaps be less anxious.

151

Outdoors, this older child is a dynamo. He really

needs to exercise those growing muscles, and he is compelled to do this. He leaps onto his favorite vehicle—trike, bike, or scooter—and tears off to find his friends (don't let him out of sight!). He climbs trees or the jungle gym in the park and makes up games about flying in airplanes or climbing mountains. He not only masters the see-saw (with a buddy), but views *walking* it as his greatest feat (it *is* pretty good).

At a quieter moment, when he seems to have gotten rid of some of his energy, take a walk with him. He's interested in learning his neighborhood —the way to the candy store, which street runs into which other, and who lives where. He's interested, too, in learning about nature. If you bring along a jar, you can collect specimens for exhibit at home—rocks, moss, bark, leaves, perhaps even a few six- or eight-legged fellows (though not too many of these, lest the population get out of hand, not to mention the jar).

Playing should be the best part of babysitting. It's the best part of life! Use the above suggestions as starting points for your own ideas for different ages. Dip into your own imagination and experience.

9.

FIRST AID/ EMERGENCIES

In your entire babysitting career you may never have to deal with a mishap more serious than a scraped knee or a burned-out light bulb. The odds are in your favor. At a scary moment, though, you might be confronted with a situation that demands your quick and sensible action. It is most important, even if you are frightened, for you to remain calm. If you don't know what to do, it's far better that you take a minute to read a paragraph or two of advice than to run around in a panic doing the wrong things. Your own calmness in an emergency situation will greatly comfort and reassure a child who is frightened or in pain.

This chapter will give you the information you need to deal with the *onset* of emergencies. Your job is to get in expert help as quickly as possible and, in the meantime, keep matters from worsening until help arrives. The first and longest section gives you first-aid procedures for physical injuries

153

and illnesses. The second tells you how to deal with other, more general types of bad luck.

FIRST AID

Your goal, of course, is to keep the child safe from accidents, but even with the best of care children sometimes get hurt. Usually, the hurt is a little one, a mosquito bite or a stubbed toe that can be made "all better" with a kiss or a Band-Aid and the assurance that it will soon be well. Occasionally, too, a child may come down with symptoms of illness while in your care. In these cases, the better part of first aid is simply good cheer. Cuddle him. Calm his fears. Do whatever you can to keep him distracted from his discomfort.

Most children, when hurt or ill, desperately want their parents. Whether or not the situation calls for the parents' immediate return depends on individual circumstances. Your judgment will prevail here. In any case, a child deserves all your attention and tenderness until he feels fine again or until his parents get home.

The following are directions for dealing with common childhood injuries and ailments. For the simple kind, you are told how to administer minor first-aid procedures. For serious cases, you are told how to keep the child comfortable and his condition stable, and where to get help.

No attempt is made here to teach the use of splints or slings, artificial respiration, or the application of a tourniquet. Experience shows that such techniques are best learned in a classroom where they can be demonstrated by a licensed instructor and practiced by the students. Knowledge of first aid is a valuable asset in general, not just in babysitting. It would be wise for you to take a course

155

at your high school or college, community center,
or the American Red Cross. Both the Boy Scouts
and Girl Scouts offer badges in first aid.

Getting Help

Always, always inform the parents of any injury
or onset of illness—immediately if serious, otherwise when they come home. If you decide to telephone them right away, describe calmly exactly
what has happened, the severity of the situation,
and what you have done so far. Be prepared to
follow further instructions. Have handy paper and
pencil and your list of emergency telephone numbers. If for some reason you are unable to reach
the parents, you will need to resort to other help
or advice—from a nearby friend or relative, the
pediatrician or hospital. In a situation in which
you think the child's life or limb is threatened, get
medical help first. Telephone the parents afterward.

If *you* are injured or become ill on the job, give
yourself first aid as described on the following
pages. If you feel that your ability to take care of
the child is impaired or that you need to go home
or to see a doctor immediately, by all means leave.
Get someone else to take over for you—a nearby
friend or relative of the child's parents, someone
from your own family, or a friend of yours who
babysits. Telephone the child's parents.

Giving Medication

Never, never give any medication, not so much
as an aspirin, without specific instructions to do

156   so. If you are asked to give a child, for instance,
cough medicine before he goes to sleep or to dab
on calamine lotion for poison ivy, follow the par-

ents' instructions, preferably written, *and* read the label on the container. Give him exactly the amount indicated at exactly the right time. Immediately return the medicine to safe storage with its safety cap locked in place. Never give medicine in the dark. Never call it candy. (If a clear explanation of why he must take the medicine doesn't get him to open his mouth, ply him with the promise of a treat or some special event afterward.) Never take medication yourself in front of the child. If you have medication in your bag, put it out of his reach.

Allergic Reaction

Children can be allergic to a variety of substances, from bee venom to house dust to types of foods, such as milk, wheat, or chocolate. Reactions, which are sometimes difficult to recognize, can range from simple runny nose and sneezing to bronchial asthma (severe difficulty breathing); from a slight skin rash to hives (itchy white bumps) or eczema (itchy, rough, red patches); from crankiness to vomiting. Parents should tell you in advance about a child's allergy, so you can keep him away from the offending substance or treat his reaction to it. If an allergic reaction happens unexpectedly, call them at once for instructions. If you cannot reach them and the reaction is severe—there is vomiting or difficulty breathing —call the child's pediatrician. Give no medication without specific instructions to do so. You can make an itching child somewhat more comfortable by bathing him with warm water and baking soda: one cupful of soda to a small tub of water, two cups to a large tub. (See *Breathing Difficulty*, p. 160; *Rash*, p. 174; *Sting, Insect*, p. 176; and *Vomiting*, p. 178.)

157

Back Injury (See *Spinal Injury,* p. 175)

Bite, Animal or Human

If the skin is punctured or torn, wash the wound immediately with soap and water. Dry with clean cloth or gauze. Put on Band-Aid or gauze bandage. If this is only a nip from a sib or the family pet and the wound is minor, you can wait to tell the parents when they come home. If the bite is more serious (it is deep, or on the face or neck) or was given by a strange dog or other animal, telephone them at once.

Bleeding (Cuts and Scratches)

Ordinary bleeding from a cut or scrape can be controlled with direct pressure on the wound. First, wash with soap and water. Remove bits of dirt or other matter by holding the injured part under cool, running water. Then put direct pressure on the wound: Press the wound firmly with clean cloth or gauze. When bleeding has stopped, put on Band-Aid or gauze bandage.

Serious bleeding must be controlled immediately. Loss of half the body's blood is always fatal. Immediately telephone—or have someone else telephone—for emergency medical help. Treat for shock (see p. 174).

Try to control the bleeding first with direct pressure: Press the wound firmly with a clean cloth or pad of gauze. Whether the blood clots or soaks through, do not remove the cloth or gauze pad. Just keep the pressure and add more cloth or gauze if necessary. Unless there is a broken bone involved (see p. 161), elevate the injured part higher than the heart. If this fails to stop the bleeding—and help has not yet come—continue di-

158

rect pressure and elevation and *also* apply pressure
to the nearest artery between the wound and
heart. (See illustration.) Press firmly against the
bone:

> For a wound on the scalp or temple, press in
> front of the ear;
> for one on the face, press below the hollow
> of the jaw;

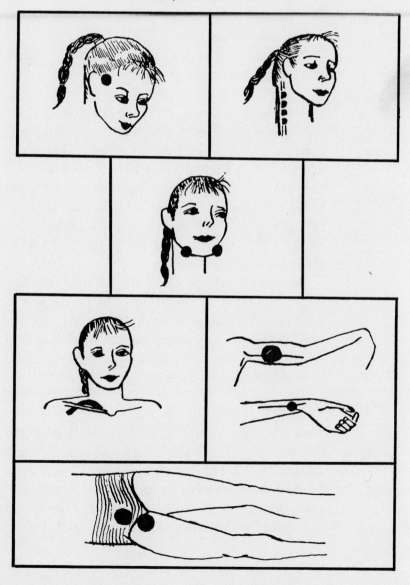

for one in the neck or throat, press to the right of the windpipe;

for one in the upper arm, armpit, or shoulder, press into the groove behind the collarbone;

for one in the lower arm or hand, press midway between elbow and armpit on the inner side of the upper arm, in the groove between the muscles;

for one in the hands or fingers, press the inside of the wrist;

for one in the leg or foot, press the inner thigh near the groin.

In very extreme cases, in which the above methods have not stopped the bleeding, a tourniquet is needed. But the use of a tourniquet is dangerous and should be limited to life-and-death situations. If medical help has not arrived *and* the situation is life-threatening *and* you have had a course in first aid and know how to apply a tourniquet, do so. Be sure to note the time you do this and tell the medical people.

Do not attempt to clean the wound. Bandage with clean cloth or gauze. Once the bandage is in place, do not remove it until medical help has arrived. When you have stopped the bleeding and treated for shock *or* the child is receiving medical help, telephone the parents.

Breathing Difficulty

Occasionally a child may take a fall that knocks the "wind" out of him. This is startling but not serious. He'll get his breath back in a few moments.

160   There are a number of serious situations, however, that cause, or can cause, critical difficulty in breathing: severe allergic reaction; head, spinal,

or chest injuries; choking; drowning; electric shock; poisoning; and suffocation. In any situation in which the child's breathing has stopped, it is crucial that he be given artificial respiration immediately. If you know how, do so. If not, waste no time getting someone on the scene who does. Call a nearby knowledgeable adult, an ambulance or rescue squad. When the child is receiving medical attention, telephone his parents.

Broken Bone (Fracture, Dislocation)

If a child has had a bad fall or wrench that is extremely painful, you must consider the possibility of a broken bone (a fracture) or a dislocation. There are two kinds of fractures, *simple* and *compound*. A simple fracture is just a broken bone—there is no wound in the skin. A compound fracture is a broken bone *with* a wound in the skin, usually caused by a jagged end of the broken bone tearing through. A compound fracture is worse than a simple one because of the greater danger of infection and shock. You must be careful how you treat a simple fracture so as not to make it compound. A dislocation is when a bone gets out of place at the joint.

Sometimes it's hard to tell if there is a broken bone or not, particularly if the fracture is simple. (See *Sprain*, p. 176.) Compare the injured part of the body to the opposite, uninjured part. If the bone is broken, there may be swelling or deformity. Very gently—because this may hurt—run your fingers over the injured area. You may be able to feel the break. The child may be able to tell you he heard or felt a snap when he was injured. He may be able to feel the broken ends grating against each other. He may be unable to move the broken part or the joint nearest it. He

161

may go into shock. A dislocation may cause many of these same symptoms, particularly intense pain and swelling at the joint and complete loss of movement. In a compound fracture, in addition to these symptoms, there will be a wound in the skin, and you may even be able to see the broken bone. The child may suffer from severe bleeding and shock.

If you think it at all likely that the child has a broken bone or dislocation, call an ambulance or doctor right away. If possible, also call in a nearby adult for advice and support. Keep the child as comfortable as possible with blankets and pillows (see *Spinal Injury*, p. 175). Treat for shock (see p. 174). Unless he is in a dangerous spot—there is a fire or other life-threatening emergency—do not move him; especially do not move his injured part. On the street, stop traffic rather than move the child. If you must move him from harm's way, try to get someone to help, and first bind the injured part as comfortably and securely as possible. It is most important to keep the injured part—and preferably his whole body—well supported, so that the move will not cause further pain or injury.

When medical aid is on the way and the child has been made as comfortable as possible, telephone the parents.

Bruising

A bruise is an area of swelling and discoloration caused by a blow. Active children get them frequently, and although bruises can be painful, usually they are not serious. (A bad bruise on the head is another matter; see *Head Injury*, p. 169). You can make the bruise less painful and keep down the swelling and discoloration by putting an ice pack or a cold cloth directly on the area just after the injury. If the skin is broken, treat as you would any cut (see *Bleeding*, p. 158).

Burns (See also *Sunburn*, p. 177)

Heat or Electrical. For *lesser* burns—first or second degree, where the skin is reddened or blistered—soak in cold (not ice) water until the pain is better. Gently blot dry. Do not put on pressure or medication of any kind. Loosely put on a sterile bandage. Telephone the parents.

For *serious* burns—third degree, where the skin is white or charred—*don't do anything to the burn.* Call an ambulance immediately. Cover the burn with clean, dry cloth or gauze—nothing that will stick to the skin. Elevate the burned part. Treat for shock (see p. 174). When medical help is on the way, telephone the parents.

Chemical. Immediately flush the area of the burn with cool running water for at least five minutes. If the chemical is over a large area, put the child under a hard-running shower or hose and remove his clothing while rinsing his body. Blot dry. Cover the burn with a clean, dry cloth or gauze—nothing that will stick to the skin. Telephone an ambulance or doctor. (If the child is old enough to run water over the burn or shower on his own, you can telephone earlier.) Treat for shock (see p. 174). When medical aid is on the way, telephone the parents.

Choking (See also *Swallowed Object*, p. 177)

163   Choking is caused when a swallowed object gets stuck in the child's throat or windpipe. His face turns red. He coughs or tries to cough. He may gag and have difficulty breathing (see p. 160). As long as he is able to get his breath and is making good

efforts of his own to get the object unstuck, leave him alone. If he is having difficulty or panicking, give him one or more sharp slaps on the back, between the shoulder blades. If this doesn't work, hold him upside down or over your arm, while slapping his back. (See illustration.) As a last resort, force your finger into his mouth to the back of the throat and try to pull the object out. If he is turning blue from lack of air, rush him to the hospital at once. Call an ambulance or nearby adult with car. Telephone parents afterward.

Cold Virus

Some children have frequent colds. There's not much you can do to cure one, but if a child comes down with symptoms—tiredness, crankiness, runny nose, watery eyes, sneezing, coughing—you should take care to keep him indoors and warm (not *overly* warm) until his parents come home. Give him rest or quiet play and plenty of fluids. If there is a vaporizer or humidifier in the house, put it on. Give him no medication without specific instructions to do so. If he gets fever (see p. 169), telephone his parents.

Convulsion

The most common cause of convulsion in small children is the onset of fever. Another cause is epilepsy. The child may fall down, twitch all over, clench his teeth, roll his eyes, froth a little at the mouth, breathe heavily, urinate or defecate, lose consciousness. It's a pretty scary thing to watch, but is not dangerous in itself and usually doesn't last long. Afterward, the child may fall asleep exhausted.

The main thing for you to do during the convulsion is keep the child from hurting himself. Remove all dangerous objects from the area. Do not restrain him, but loosen his clothing. You may want to put a pillow under his head or turn him on his side to help keep his airways open, but do not move him around unnecessarily. Give him nothing to drink while he is convulsing. Afterward put him to bed. Telephone his parents as soon as possible after he is settled. A convulsion may be the beginning of a serious illness. If he seems to have fever (see p. 169), you need not cover him with blankets but may give him a cool sponge bath (see p. 132).

Cuts, Scratches (See *Bleeding*, p. 158)

Diarrhea

Many small babies, particularly those not yet on solid foods and most particularly those who are breast-fed, have several loose bowel movements throughout the day. This is not diarrhea. Even in older babies and small children, diarrhea can be caused by nothing more than too much of a good thing to eat, such as chocolate or applesauce. Of course, it can also mark the onset of illness. If the diarrhea is profuse, contains pus or blood, or is accompanied by vomiting or fever (see pp. 178 and 169), telephone the parents. If the child wears diapers you may need to use ointment to prevent

165

rash (see p. 174). Be matter-of-fact about any mess that is made (see p. 62). Do not let the child see that you are bothered by it, even if you are.

Dislocation (See *Broken Bone*, p. 161)

Drowning

Hold the child at an angle, head down, over your knees to help drain water from his lungs and stomach. If he is able, he will cough or vomit. If he has stopped breathing (see p. 160), and you know how to administer artificial respiration, do so at once. If you don't know how, waste no time getting someone on the scene who does. Call a nearby knowledgeable adult, an ambulance, or rescue squad. When the child is receiving medical attention, telephone his parents.

Earache

Infection. When a child who has had or is getting a cold complains of an earache, either directly or by crying and rubbing his ear, it probably means he has an ear infection. Tell his parents. If he is crying a lot or if he has fever (see p. 169), telephone them immediately. In the meantime see if a heating pad or hot-water bottle (not too hot) on the ear gives him any relief. Give no medication without specific instructions to do so.

Injury. Treat a blow or cut as you would if it were on any other part of the body (see *Bruising*, p. 162, and *Bleeding*, p. 158), but treat only the *outer* ear. If injury to the eardrum seems at all likely, telephone the parents or/and take him to the pediatrician or hospital.

Foreign Object. Small children often put things like peas, pebbles, and buttons into their ears and noses (see p. 171). Don't try to remove such an object yourself. Your efforts may push it in farther. Turn the child's head to the side and down. If the object doesn't fall out, telephone the parents or/and take him to the pediatrician or hospital.

Electrical Shock

Even little jolts—say, from touching an outlet with a wet finger—can be unpleasant. A shock from a live wire can cause serious burns, unconsciousness, and death. If the child is still in contact with the wire, the situation is extremely dangerous for you as well. *Do not touch the child or the source of the shock yourself.* Try to get a nearby adult in for help. Try to shut the current off. If that's not possible, stand on something dry, like a board or stack of newspapers, and (be sure your

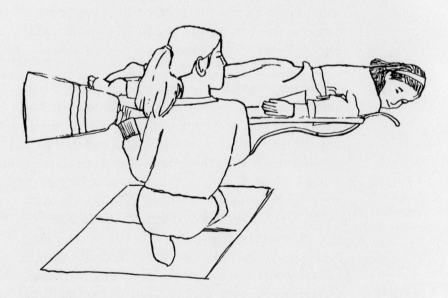

167

hands are dry) with a stick, broom handle, or piece of clothing pull the child away from the wire or the wire away from him. (See illustration.) Telephone for an ambulance or rescue squad immediately. Treat the child for shock (see p. 174 and *Burns*, p. 163). If his breathing has stopped and you know how to administer artificial respiration, do so. If you don't know how, waste no time in getting someone on the scene who does. After medical help has arrived, telephone the parents.

Eye Injury

Blows, Cuts. Treat the eyelid and area around the eye as you would any other part of the body (see *Bleeding*, p. 158, and *Bruising*, p. 162). Injury to the eyeball itself *must* be treated by a doctor. In this case, cover the eye loosely with a bandage or clean cloth. Do not allow the child to touch his eye even if you must hold or bind his hands. Take him to the pediatrician or hospital Then telephone the parents.

Foreign Body. You can attempt to remove small objects causing mild irritation. Sometimes the child's eye will tear and wash the object out. If not, see if he will let you pull the lid back and pick the object out with the corner of a clean cloth or gauze—not with your finger or any hard instrument. If he can't tolerate this, flush his eye with cold water. A stubborn object or one impaled in the eye *must* be treated by a doctor. Do nothing to the eye yourself. Do not allow the child to touch his eye even if you must hold or bind his hands. Cover loosely with a clean cloth or gauze. Take him to a pediatrician or hospital. Telephone the parents.

168

Chemical. Despite protests, hold his eyelid open and flush with cold water from faucet or hose for several minutes. Do not allow water from the affected eye to run into the other eye. Cover loosely with a clean cloth or gauze. Take him to a doctor or hospital. Telephone the parents.

Fever

You don't necessarily need to take a child's temperature to know he has fever. He will seem out of sorts and feel overly warm to the touch. If the fever is moderately high or high, 101 degrees or more, he will be flushed and glassy-eyed. He may show other signs of illness, such as runny nose or diarrhea. Telephone his parents at once. While waiting for their return, you can keep his fever down with a lukewarm, not cold, bath or sponge bath (see p. 132) if they want you to do this. Avoid drafts and chilling. Give no medication without specific instructions to do so. (See *Convulsions*, p. 164.)

Fracture (See *Broken Bone*, p. 161)

Head Injury

Blow. Toddlers and small children bump their heads frequently. As long as the child stops crying within several minutes, he's probably all right. If he has an "egg" on his head, treat it as you would any bruise (see p. 162), then let him go about his business. However, if he shows any of the following signs of serious head injury, telephone his parents and pediatrician or hospital immediately: unconsciousness (see p. 178), difficulty with breathing (see p. 160) or vision, pupils unequal in size, vomiting (see p. 178), convulsions (see p. 164), paralysis. Keep him lying quietly until help

169

arrives. Put ice pack or cold cloth on the bump, but no pressure. Treat for shock.

Cut. For a minor cut, control bleeding with direct, but not heavy, pressure. Clean and bandage the wound. Keep the child quiet until he seems fine again.

For more severe bleeding, raise the child's head and shoulders higher than his heart, but do not bend his neck. Consider the possibility of a spinal injury (see p. 175). If bleeding is alarmingly severe, apply pressure to nearest artery (see illustration on p. 159). Treat for shock (see p. 174). Telephone pediatrician or hospital, then the parents.

Mouth Injury

Be sure that there are no other, more serious head or spinal injuries (see pp. 169 and 175). Reduce the pain and swelling of a bruised, or "fat," lip, by putting on an ice pack or cold cloth. You can stop bleeding of lips, tongue, gums or palate by direct, gentle pressure (see p. 158). When the bleeding has stopped, you can ease his pain by giving the child small slivers of crushed ice to suck.

If a tooth has been knocked out, pack the bleeding socket with a clean cloth or gauze. Save the tooth for possible implant. Telephone the parents.

Neck Injury (See *Spinal Injury*, p. 175)

Nose Injury

Nosebleed. Bleeding from a minor injury or sinus infection can be controlled by putting an ice pack or a cold cloth on the bridge of the nose and gently pinching the nostrils together. If bleeding has not stopped in five or ten minutes, gently pack the nostril(s) with cotton or gauze and try pinching again. When bleeding has stopped, the child can resume play, but do not allow him to blow his nose for several hours. If the bleeding continues or recurs, telephone the parents, pediatrician, or hospital.

Broken Nose. Treat bleeding as above. Telephone pediatrician or hospital, parents.

Foreign Object. Don't try to remove the object yourself. Your attempts may push it in farther. Have the child hold his head upright or tilted slightly forward and blow through both nostrils. If the object does not come out this way, telephone his parents.

Poisoning

Poisoning is the most common cause of accidental death in young children. It seems to happen most frequently when children are hungry or thirsty. Take note, too, that if a child has *ever* attempted to swallow a poison, he is apt to try it again if he has the opportunity.

If you know or if you think the child has just swallowed a poisonous substance (see partial list below) or if you find any of the symptoms of poisoning (also listed below), call the poison control center, pediatrician, or hospital. Tell them what the child has swallowed or what you think he has swallowed, his symptoms (if any—don't wait for them to appear), and his age. They will tell you what to do. Unless you are knowledgeable about the types of poisons, their symptoms, and effects on the body, do not attempt any remedy yourself, *except*—and only if the child is conscious—to give him plenty of milk or water to drink. If you are unable to get information by telephone within

171

minutes, waste no time getting the child to the nearest emergency room. Call an ambulance, rescue squad, or nearby adult with car. Take with you the remains of the substance swallowed, the container, or a sample of the child's vomitus. Call the parents from the hospital.

SOME POISONOUS SUBSTANCES

alcohol

ammonia

antifreeze

antihistamines

aspirin

birth-control pills and
  creams

bleach

bug spray

cleaners, liquid and
  powder

cologne

cosmetics

deodorant and room
  deodorizers

detergent

dishwasher granules

drain cleaner

dry-cleaning fluid

fabric softener

fingernail polish and
  remover

gasoline

hair care products

indelible markers

iodine

iron tablets

kerosene

lighter fluid

lye

mothballs

oven cleaner

pain killers

paint and paint
  thinner

perfume

pesticides

plants (see below)

polish and wax

suntan lotion

toiletries

tranquilizers

turpentine

weed killers

SOME SYMPTOMS OF SWALLOWED POISONING

Telltale stains or odors on the child's clothes or skin

Container open or out of place

Burns on throat, mouth, hands

Sudden changes in behavior, such as drowsiness, stomach pain, irritability, overactivity, fear

Nausea and/or vomiting

Thirst

Cold sweats

Difficulty breathing

Unconsciousness

Convulsions

Chemical Burns (See *Burns*, p. 163)

Inhaled Poisons. Fumes from car exhaust or from chemicals such as cleaner or paint thinner can cause irritation of mucous membranes and body linings, headache, nausea, shortness of breath, dizziness, unconsciousness, or convulsions. Get the child to fresh air; keep him warm. Call poison control, the pediatrician, or hospital. Then telephone the parents.

Poisonous Plants. You'd have to be a botanist to know them all, but below is a partial list. Some are poisonous only if swallowed; others cause irritation on contact with the skin. If you find the child has swallowed parts of a poisonous plant, or suspect that he has, call poison control, the pediatrician, or the hospital. If in doubt about a plant, call. React as you would for any swallowed poison (see above). If he has touched the leaves of poison ivy or the like, remove his clothing and bathe him with soap and warm water. Call poison control,

173

the pediatrician, or hospital for further instructions. Telephone his parents.

Some Poisonous Plants

African Violet	Poinsettia
Baneberry	Poison Hemlock
Begonia	Poison Ivy
Bittersweet	Poison Oak
Castor Bean	Poison Sumac
Dieffenbachia	Pokeweed
Jimson Weed	Water Hemlock
Larkspur	Yew
Lily-of-the-Valley	

Rash

Children are susceptible to all kinds of rashes, the most common being allergic hives or eczema (see p. 157), diaper rash (see p. 121), and prickly heat (a hot-weather reaction usually on the shoulders and neck). Other rashes—bumps, pimples, and so forth—can be symptoms of contagious disease. Usually these are accompanied by fever and other signs of illness, but sometimes not. Never give medication without specific instructions to do so. Do tell the parents about any rash you find. If the child seems itchy and uncomfortable, a bath in warm water and baking soda (one cup to a small tub, two cups to a large tub) can't hurt. If you suspect illness or that the child is suffering an outbreak of poison ivy or the like (see p. 173), telephone the parents.

Shock

Any serious injury, called a "trauma," especially

one involving bleeding, broken bones, burns, or poisoning, can lead to shock; and shock can kill just as surely as the injury itself. The symptoms are splotchy or pale, moist skin; shallow or irregular breathing; rapid, weak pulse; chills; drooping eyelids, dilated pupils; nausea and/or vomiting; collapse; mental confusion. *Always* treat the seriously injured child for shock. Watch for it even with minor injuries.

TREATMENT FOR SHOCK

1. After any bleeding is under control, or if possible, during the attempt to stop it, have the child lie down. In the aftermath of many injuries he will already be lying down, in which case do not move him, especially if you suspect a broken bone, or head or spinal injury.

2. Place blankets over and, if he can be moved and the ground is cold or damp, under him. Do not have him overheated. The object is to keep his body temperature normal.

3. Prop his feet a little higher than his head unless this causes pain or breathing difficulty. Again, if you suspect a broken bone, or head or spinal injury, do not prop his feet or move him.

4. Give nothing by mouth.

5. Telephone ambulance, pediatrician, or hospital.

Spinal Injury

The symptoms of a broken or dislocated neck or back are: body alignment askew; pain in the neck or back; inability to move hands or feet. If you suspect a spinal injury, *do not move the child or twist his body in any way*. Do not even let him raise his head. Immobilize his body in the position you found it by bracing his neck and back with

175

rolled up blankets, towels, or clothing. Treat for shock (see p. 174). Telephone for an ambulance or rescue squad. When medical help is on the way, telephone the parents.

Splinter

Wash the area with soap and warm water. Continue to soak in warm water for a few minutes to soften the skin. Remove splinter with sterile tweezers or needle.

Sprain

A sprain is a dislocation, but in this case the bone goes right back into place again. Sprains happen most often to wrists or ankles. Symptoms are: intense pain at the joint; immediate swelling; inability to move the part without additional pain; and, later, a bruise that may last for weeks. Elevate the sprained part. Put on ice packs or cold compresses. (Never put ice or ice water directly on the skin.) Some sprains are minor—the child is using the part again shortly. If the sprain is severe—very painful and swollen—call the parents. It is likely that they'll want the limb x-rayed. Sometimes a sprain is hard to tell from a broken bone or dislocation (see p. 161). If in doubt, treat for the more serious injury.

Sting, Insect

Ordinary bites from such insects as fleas, flies, and mosquitoes can be simply washed with soap and water. You can put on a paste of baking soda and water to stop the itching. For bee stings (wasp, hornet, or yellow jacket) and spider bites, do the same but also put an ice pack on the sting. If he has only one sting, just keep the child quiet for a while and watch for a severe reaction, particularly if he has allergies. If he has many stings *or* if he gets such symptoms as severe pain, swelling (anywhere in the body), sweats, nausea, or muscle cramps, difficulty in breathing, shock, or unconsciousness, get him to a pediatrician or hospital immediately. Call an ambulance, rescue squad, or nearby adult with car. Telephone the parents afterward.

Suffocation (See also *Breathing Difficulty*, p. 160, and *Unconsciousness*, p. 178)

Get the child to fresh air. Loosen his clothing. Keep him warm. If breathing has stopped and you know how to give artificial respiration, do so at once. If you don't know how, waste no time getting someone on the scene who does. Call a nearby knowledgeable adult, ambulance, or rescue squad. Telephone the parents afterward.

Sunburn

A fair-skinned child unused to the sun should not be exposed to direct sunlight for more than a few minutes. If he is, be sure that his skin is protected by sunhat, long sleeves, and long pants. Don't trust suntan lotions to keep out harmful rays. (Note, also, that many of these are poisonous if swallowed; see p. 171.) If he does get sunburned or if you find him sunburned when you arrive, you can make him a little more comfortable with cold cream or lotion. If he develops chills or fever or feels sickish, telephone his parents at once. A sunburn can be as dangerous as any other type of burn.

Swallowed Objects (See also *Choking*, p. 163)

177   As long as the button, penny, pebble, or whatever gets down without causing choking or other

injury, there is a very good chance that the child's digestive system will eliminate it in the normal course of things. Do tell the parents when they return so they can watch for symptoms of intestinal obstruction. If he swallows a sharp object, such as a needle, call them at once. They will want to consult the pediatrician.

Unconsciousness

If you know the *cause* of the child's unconsciousness—electrical shock (see p. 167), poisoning (see p. 171), head injury (see p. 169), etc. —refer to that section of the first-aid information. If you don't know the cause, check the color of the face: If his face is red, put him in a lying down position, head and shoulders slightly raised. Loosen the clothing around his neck and put an ice pack or cold cloth on his forehead. If his face is white, move him as little as possible and treat for shock (see p. 174). If his face is blue, he will need artificial respiration. If you know how, do it at once. If you don't know, waste no time in getting someone on the scene who does. In any case of unconsciousness, get medical help as soon as possible. Telephone the parents afterward.

Vomiting

Vomiting, particularly the mild spit-up type, can simply be a baby's or young child's way of ridding his sensitive stomach of sour contents. It can also be a symptom of illness or poisoning (see p. 171). If the child vomits only once with no other symptoms, assume the first explanation, but tell his parents when they return. Clean the mess (see p. 62) matter-of-factly; don't let him see that you are bothered by it even if you are. Keep him quiet for a while to be sure he's all right.

178

Until you are sure, give him nothing by mouth except a little crushed ice or a lollipop. If he vomits again *or* shows any other signs of illness (fever, pain, diarrhea, etc.), call his parents. Give no medication without specific instructions to do so.

OTHER EMERGENCIES

Fire or Smoke

If you discover fire or heavy smoke, get yourself and the child out of the house immediately. Do not hang around to assess the situation or attempt to put out the fire yourself. Don't bother to dress or stop to make a phone call. Get to the nearest neighbor and telephone the fire department from there. Telephone the parents next.

Flood (See also *Plumbing*, p. 57)

Water on the floor becomes dangerous when it reaches electrical wiring or if the floor begins to collapse. Don't wait for this to happen. If the situation looks like it might get out of hand, get yourself and the child out of the house. Get to the nearest neighbor and telephone the fire department from there. Telephone the parents next.

Gas Leak

Escaping gas can be hard to smell if the leak is small and especially if you've been in the room with it all along, but it can be quite dangerous. Over a period of time it can cause unconsciousness and death or, if ignited, an explosion. If you smell gas and cannot immediately find its source to turn it off (like a jet on the range left slightly askew), get yourself and the child out of the

179

house. Go to the building superintendent or, if you're in a private house, to the nearest neighbor. If the adult is able to locate the leak and turn it off, afterward just open the windows and air out the house. Otherwise, telephone the power company.

Nuisance Call

If you are ever frightened or annoyed by a telephone call—the caller speaks maliciously or obscenely to you or just breathes—hang up. Don't talk, because that's what the caller wants. If you get more than one call and/or you are made nervous, telephone a member of your family to come and stay with you until the parents return *or* telephone the parents and ask them to return as soon as possible. If you feel an immediate physical threat, telephone the police. By all means tell the parents when they return about any nuisance call you received, whether or not you were bothered by it. They may want to notify the telephone company.

Power Failure (See also *Lights*, p. 56)

You need not be alarmed if, because of a shortage or a violent storm, there is a blackout in your neighborhood. It's certainly possible to do just fine without electricity for a number of hours. If it is daylight, the child probably will not even notice. If it is dark, you may have to reassure him that all is well and that the lights will come back on eventually. Be calm and matter-of-fact about the situation. Make it a small adventure.

First, get out flashlight, lantern, or candles. If you are using a lantern or candles, be sure you place them on a level surface where they cannot be knocked over. Always put candles in holders or

180

saucers to prevent accidental fire. Telephone the power company. If a large area is blacked out, they probably will know already, but do it anyway. Telephone the parents. They may decide to come home. Then, just stay indoors and as much as possible go about business as usual. Do not allow a child to roughhouse in the dark. Do not do anything in the kitchen or bathroom without enough light for safety. Try not to open the refrigerator, especially the freezer compartment, until the power comes back on.

Prowler

Be assured that it is entirely normal to sometimes have uneasy feelings in someone else's home late at night. This is due to the strangeness of your surroundings and possibly to the vividness of your imagination. If you think you're just nervous, telephone an adult to come over and stay with you until the parents come home. However, if you really do suspect a prowler—you hear noises at a door or window or you actually see someone—call the police at once. Give them your location and tell them, as calmly and accurately as possible, what you have heard or seen, including, if you can, a description of the prowler. It is helpful to police to be told not only an individual's height, weight, and complexion, but dress, movements, and any peculiarities you may note, such as jewelry or a limp. If you see the person leave, note the direction taken and, if there was a car, give a description of it, too. If you can't get the whole license number, try to get the first digits. In the meantime, call a nearby adult to stay with you until the police arrive.

181

10. SITTER'S LOG

This last chapter is yours to write. It is a kind of diary, a permanent record of your work. Use a double page for each job. Most of the information you will need can be gotten while you are interviewing parents before or during the first visit.

Try to be especially conscientious about filling in the emergency telephone numbers (do this in ink). It will take only a few minutes, you'll never have to do it again, and, if you should ever need them, you'll be thankful that they're there. Parents (your own as well as the ones you sit for) will appreciate your attention to this.

The other notes—on meals, bedtime, and so forth—can be taken in detail or not, depending on your experience and memory. These things tend to change as a child grows, so you may want to write in pencil. Some notes you may want to write to yourself later, as you get to know a child and his household better.

Use your calendar for appointments (see p. 29) as a financial ledger. After each job, write in the amount of money you have earned. At the end of a year, you will know exactly how much you've made, on which jobs, on which days of the week, over what period of time. This will help you plan your work—fees, schedules, etc.—in the future.

Child(ren)'s Names and Ages: _____ ,____ ;

_____ ,____ ;

_____ ,____

Parents' Names: _____

Address: _____ Phone number:_____

EMERGENCY TELEPHONE NUMBERS

Fire: _____

Police: _____

Poison Control: _____

Pediatrician: (office) _____ ;

(home) _____

Hospital (PEDIATRIC EMERGENCY NO.): _____

Ambulance or Rescue Squad: _____

Helpful Neighbor(s): (name) _____

(no.) _____ ;

(name) _____

(no.) _____

Taxi: _____

NOTES

Meal(s) and/or Snack(s)—time(s) and preference(s):

Bath—time(s) and routine(s):

Bed—time(s) and routine(s):

Play—favorite toys, games:

Special Instructions—allergies, TV rules, etc.:

Other:

Child(ren)'s Names and Ages: _____,___;

_____,___;

_____,___

Parents' Names: _____

Address: _____ Phone number:_____

EMERGENCY TELEPHONE NUMBERS

Fire: _____

Police: _____

Poison Control: _____ _____

Pediatrician: (office) _____;

(home) _____

Hospital (PEDIATRIC EMERGENCY NO.): _____

Ambulance or Rescue Squad: _____

Helpful Neighbor(s): (name) _____

(no.) _____;

(name) _____

(no.) _____

Taxi: _____

NOTES

Meal(s) and/or Snack(s)—time(s) and preference(s):

Bath—time(s) and routine(s):

Bed—time(s) and routine(s):

Play—favorite toys, games:

Special Instructions—allergies, TV rules, etc.:

Other:

Child(ren)'s Names and Ages: _____,____;

_____,____;

_____,____

Parents' Names: _____

Address: _____ Phone number:_____

EMERGENCY TELEPHONE NUMBERS

Fire: _____

Police: _____

Poison Control: _____

Pediatrician: (office) _____;

(home) _____

Hospital (PEDIATRIC EMERGENCY NO.): _____

Ambulance or Rescue Squad: _____

Helpful Neighbor(s): (name) _____

(no.) _____;

(name) _____

(no.) _____

Taxi: _____

NOTES

Meal(s) and/or Snack(s)—time(s) and preference(s):

Bath—time(s) and routine(s):

Bed—time(s) and routine(s):

Play—favorite toys, games:

Special Instructions—allergies, TV rules, etc.:

Other:

Child(ren)'s Names and Ages: _____,___;

_____,___;

_____,___

Parents' Names: _____

Address: _____ Phone number:_____

EMERGENCY TELEPHONE NUMBERS

Fire: _____

Police: _____

Poison Control: _____

Pediatrician: (office) _____;

(home) _____

Hospital (PEDIATRIC EMERGENCY NO.): _____

Ambulance or Rescue Squad: _____

Helpful Neighbor(s): (name) _____

(no.) _____;

(name) _____

(no.) _____

Taxi: _____

NOTES

Meal(s) and/or Snack(s)—time(s) and preference(s):

Bath—time(s) and routine(s):

Bed—time(s) and routine(s):

Play—favorite toys, games:

Special Instructions—allergies, TV rules, etc.:

Other:

Child(ren)'s Names and Ages: _____,____;

_____,____;

_____,___

Parents' Names: _____

Address: _____ Phone number:_____

EMERGENCY TELEPHONE NUMBERS

Fire: _____

Police: _____

Poison Control: _____

Pediatrician: (office) _____;

(home) _____

Hospital (PEDIATRIC EMERGENCY NO.): _____

Ambulance or Rescue Squad: _____

Helpful Neighbor(s): (name) _____

(no.) _____;

(name) _____

(no.) _____

Taxi: _____

NOTES

Meal(s) and/or Snack(s)—time(s) and preference(s):

Bath—time(s) and routine(s):

Bed—time(s) and routine(s):

Play—favorite toys, games:

Special Instructions—allergies, TV rules, etc.:

Other:

Child(ren)'s Names and Ages: ——————,——;

——————————————————,——;

——————————————————,——

Parents' Names: ——————————————

Address: ——————— Phone number:———

EMERGENCY TELEPHONE NUMBERS

Fire: ————————————————

Police: ———————————————

Poison Control: ——————————————

Pediatrician: (office) ————————————;

(home) ———————————

Hospital (PEDIATRIC EMERGENCY NO.): ————————

Ambulance or Rescue Squad: ——————————

Helpful Neighbor(s): (name) ————————————

(no.) —————————————;

(name) ——————————————

(no.) ——————————————

Taxi: ————————————————

NOTES

Meal(s) and/or Snack(s)—time(s) and preference(s):

Bath—time(s) and routine(s):

Bed—time(s) and routine(s):

Play—favorite toys, games:

Special Instructions—allergies, TV rules, etc.:

Other:

Child(ren)'s Names and Ages: _____ ,____;

_____ ,____;

_____ ,

Parents' Names: _____

Address: _____ Phone number:_____

EMERGENCY TELEPHONE NUMBERS

Fire: _____

Police: _____

Poison Control: _____

Pediatrician: (office) _____ ;

(home) _____

Hospital (PEDIATRIC EMERGENCY NO.): _____

Ambulance or Rescue Squad: _____

Helpful Neighbor(s): (name) _____

(no.) _____ ;

(name) _____

(no.) _____

Taxi: _____

NOTES

Meal(s) and/or Snack(s)—time(s) and preference(s):

Bath—time(s) and routine(s):

Bed—time(s) and routine(s):

Play—favorite toys, games:

Special Instructions—allergies, TV rules, etc.:

Other:

Child(ren)'s Names and Ages: _____,___;

_____,___;

_____,___

Parents' Names: _____

Address: _____ Phone number:___

EMERGENCY TELEPHONE NUMBERS

Fire: _____

Police: _____

Poison Control: _____

Pediatrician: (office) _____;

(home) _____

Hospital (PEDIATRIC EMERGENCY NO.): _____

Ambulance or Rescue Squad: _____

Helpful Neighbor(s): (name) _____

(no.) _____;

(name) _____

(no.) _____

Taxi: _____

NOTES

Meal(s) and/or Snack(s)—time(s) and preference(s):

Bath—time(s) and routine(s):

Bed—time(s) and routine(s):

Play—favorite toys, games:

Special Instructions—allergies, TV rules, etc.:

Other:

Child(ren)'s Names and Ages: _____,___;

_____,___;

_____,___

Parents' Names: _____

Address: _____ Phone number:_____

EMERGENCY TELEPHONE NUMBERS

Fire: _____

Police: _____

Poison Control: _____

Pediatrician: (office) _____;

(home) _____

Hospital (PEDIATRIC EMERGENCY NO.): _____

Ambulance or Rescue Squad: _____

Helpful Neighbor(s): (name) _____

(no.) _____;

(name) _____

(no.) _____

Taxi: _____

NOTES

Meal(s) and/or Snack(s)—time(s) and preference(s):

Bath—time(s) and routine(s):

Bed—time(s) and routine(s):

Play—favorite toys, games:

Special Instructions—allergies, TV rules, etc.:

Other:

Child(ren)'s Names and Ages: _____,____;

_____,____;

_____,____

Parents' Names: _____

Address: _____ Phone number:_____

EMERGENCY TELEPHONE NUMBERS

Fire: _____

Police: _____

Poison Control: _____

Pediatrician: (office) _____;

(home) _____

Hospital (PEDIATRIC EMERGENCY NO.): _____

Ambulance or Rescue Squad: _____

Helpful Neighbor(s): (name) _____

(no.) _____;

(name) _____

(no.) _____

Taxi: _____

NOTES

Meal(s) and/or Snack(s)—time(s) and preference(s):

Bath—time(s) and routine(s):

Bed—time(s) and routine(s):

Play—favorite toys, games:

Special Instructions—allergies, TV rules, etc.:

Other:

Child(ren)'s Names and Ages: _____,____;

_____,____;

_____,

Parents' Names: _____

Address: _____ Phone number:_____

EMERGENCY TELEPHONE NUMBERS

Fire: _____

Police: _____

Poison Control: _____

Pediatrician: (office) _____;

(home) _____

Hospital (PEDIATRIC EMERGENCY NO.): _____

Ambulance or Rescue Squad: _____

Helpful Neighbor(s): (name) _____

(no.) _____;

(name) _____

(no.) _____

Taxi: _____

NOTES

Meal(s) and/or Snack(s)—time(s) and preference(s):

Bath time(s) and routine(s):

Bed—time(s) and routine(s):

Play—favorite toys, games:

Special Instructions—allergies, TV rules, etc.:

Other:

Child(ren)'s Names and Ages: _____,____;

_____,____;

_____,

Parents' Names: _____

Address: _____ Phone number:_____

EMERGENCY TELEPHONE NUMBERS

Fire: _____

Police: _____

Poison Control: _____

Pediatrician: (office) _____;

(home) _____

Hospital (PEDIATRIC EMERGENCY NO.): _____

Ambulance or Rescue Squad: _____

Helpful Neighbor(s): (name) _____

(no.) _____;

(name) _____

(no.) _____

Taxi: _____

NOTES

Meal(s) and/or Snack(s)—time(s) and preference(s):

Bath—time(s) and routine(s):

Bed—time(s) and routine(s):

Play—favorite toys, games:

Special Instructions—allergies, TV rules, etc.:

Other:

Child(ren)'s Names and Ages: _____,____;

_____,____;

_____,____

Parents' Names: _____

Address: _____ Phone number:_____

EMERGENCY TELEPHONE NUMBERS

Fire: _____

Police: _____

Poison Control: _____

Pediatrician: (office) _____;

(home) _____

Hospital (PEDIATRIC EMERGENCY NO.): _____

Ambulance or Rescue Squad: _____

Helpful Neighbor(s): (name) _____

(no.) _____;

(name) _____

(no.) _____

Taxi: _____

NOTES

Meal(s) and/or Snack(s)—time(s) and preference(s):

Bath—time(s) and routine(s):

Bed—time(s) and routine(s):

Play—favorite toys, games:

Special Instructions—allergies, TV rules, etc.:

Other:

Child(ren)'s Names and Ages: _____,____;

_____,____;

_____,

Parents' Names: _____

Address: _____ Phone number:_____

EMERGENCY TELEPHONE NUMBERS

Fire: _____

Police: _____

Poison Control: _____

Pediatrician: (office) _____;

(home) _____

Hospital (PEDIATRIC EMERGENCY NO.): _____

Ambulance or Rescue Squad: _____

Helpful Neighbor(s): (name) _____

(no.) _____;

(name) _____

(no.) _____

Taxi: _____

INDEX

211

Index

Index

ABOUT THE AUTHOR

Barbara Benton was born in Durham, NC, and spent part of her childhood in Japan and Germany. In addition to earning a degree from Western Carolina University, where she studied early childhood education, she also did graduate work in clinical psychology at the New School for Social Research. She has worked for several publishers and now is a freelance photographer and writer. She lives in New York with her husband, son, and two stepdaughters.